ENCOURAGEMENT

Coloring Patterns to Inspire
Lovink Coloring Books

we can do small things with great LOVE.

Mother Teresa

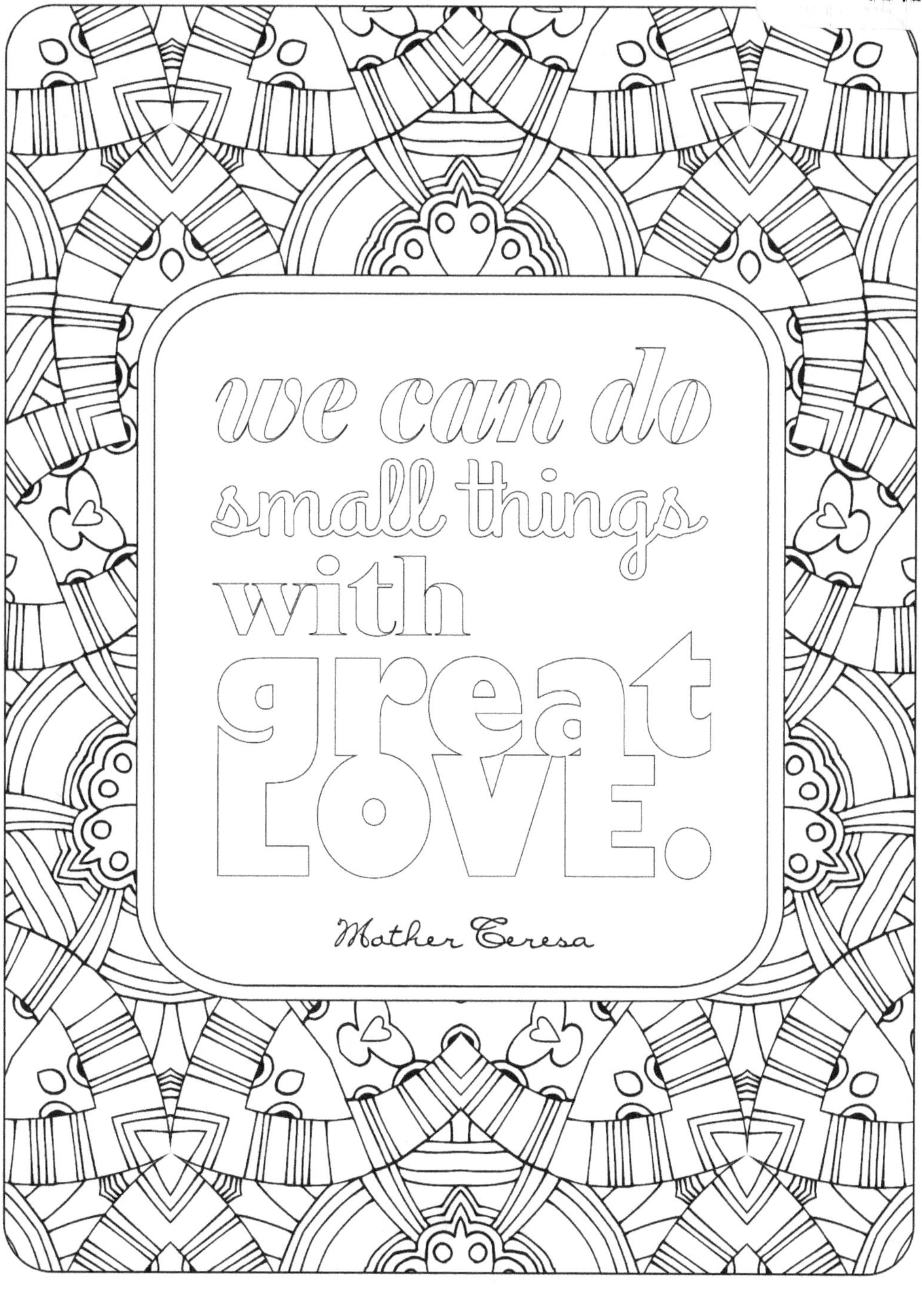

Joan Smith

Steps to a Relaxing Coloring

As an adult, you can enjoy coloring just as much as you did as a child. To make it a *truly relaxing experience*, try following these steps:

1. Find a quiet space. It's easier to focus on what you are doing when there are no distraction.

2. Organize your materials. Lay out your coloring book and crayons or pens.

3. Set the mood. Turn on some tranquil music, diffuse lavender or another relaxing oil and make sure you have your preferred drink at hand.

4. Select your picture. Which image speaks to you today? That's the one you should color.

5. Choose your palette. Select the colors you will be using for your image.

6. Begin coloring. This is the fun part. Don't worry about getting everything perfect, just start.

Allow yourself to relax and focus on the coloring. You'll find it is an amazing way to alleviate stress and take a little time out from the day's hassles. If you feel don't want to do it anymore, just stop!

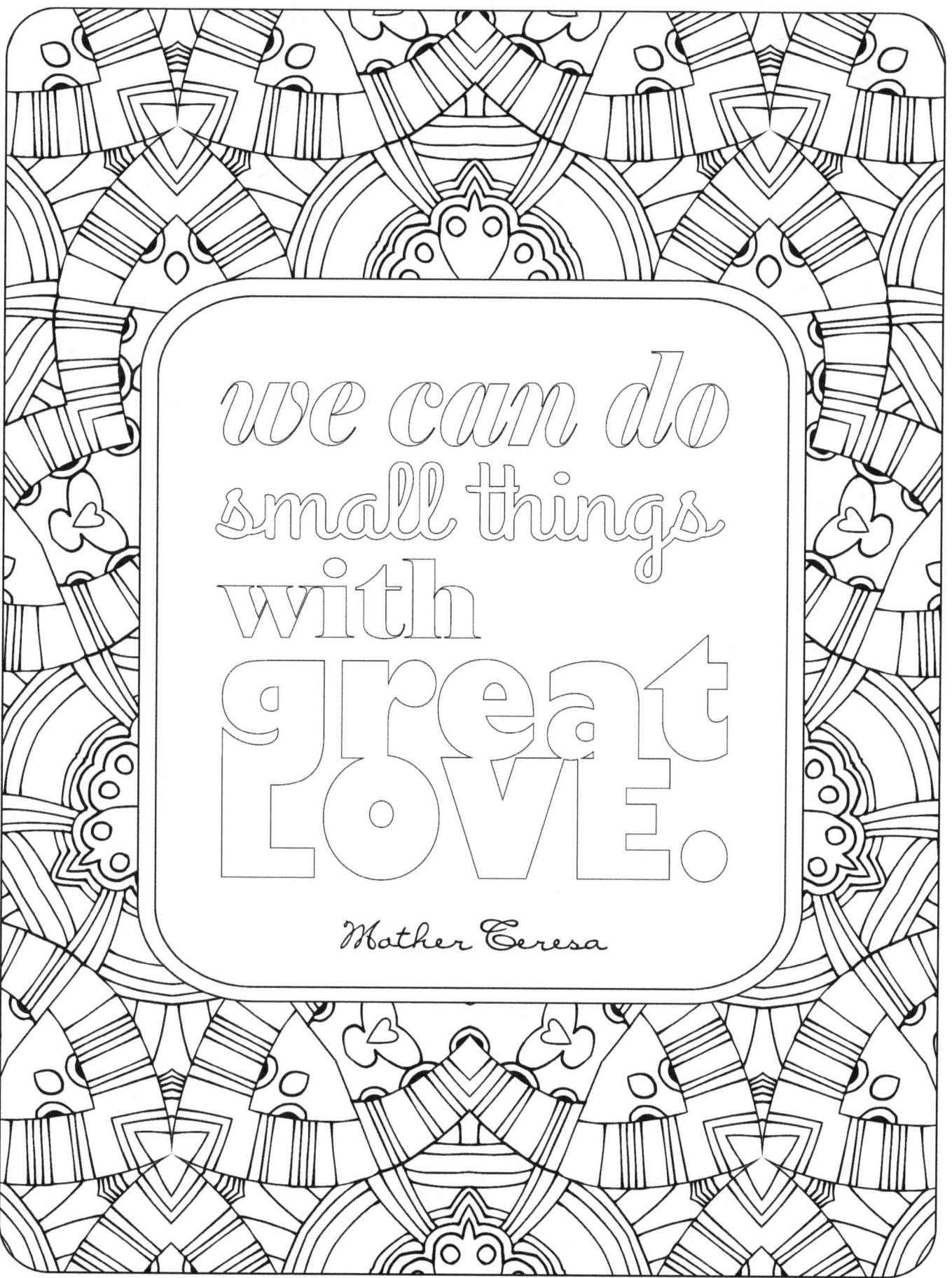

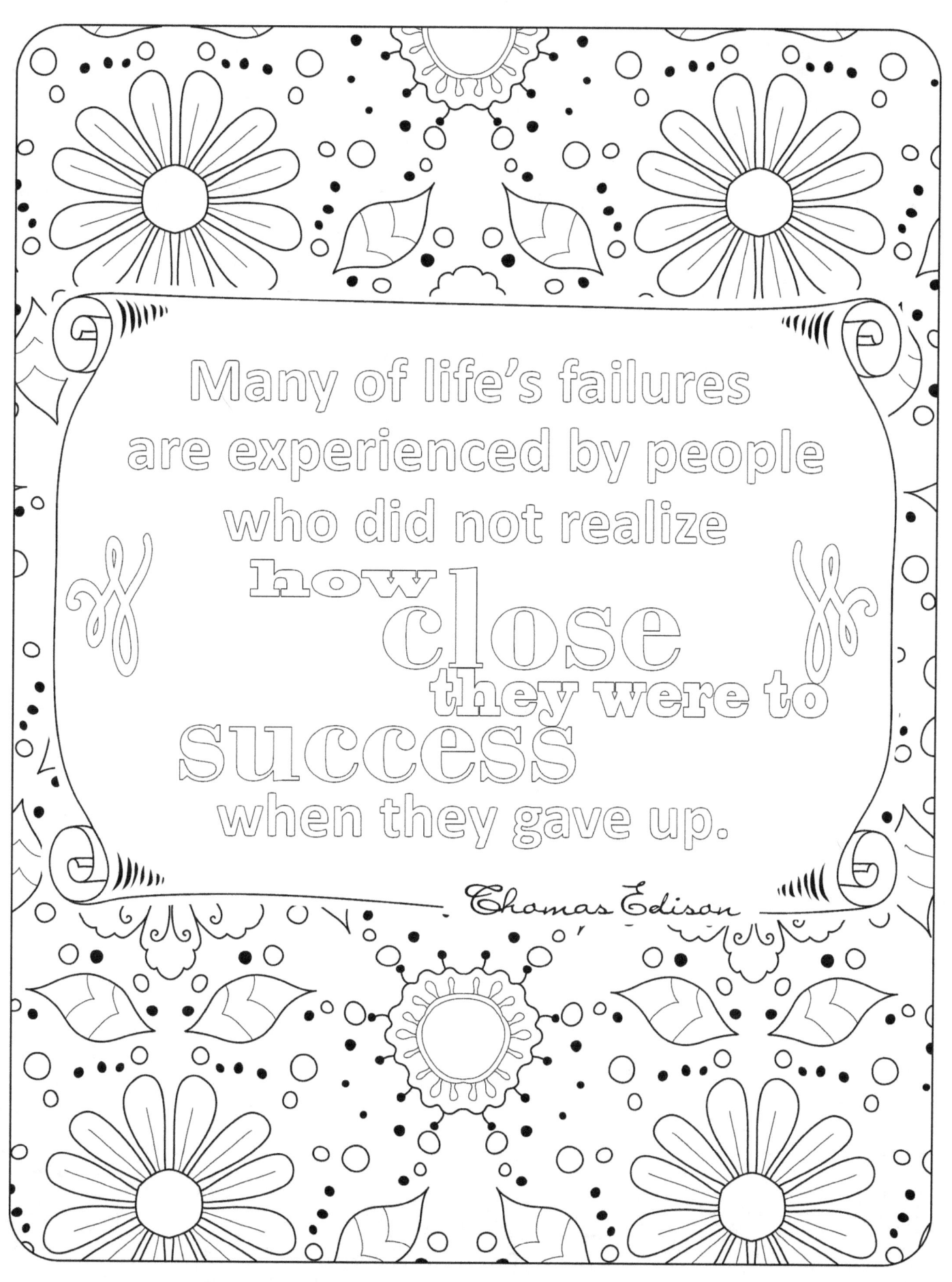

Many of life's failures
are experienced by people
who did not realize
how
close
they were to
success
when they gave up.

— Thomas Edison

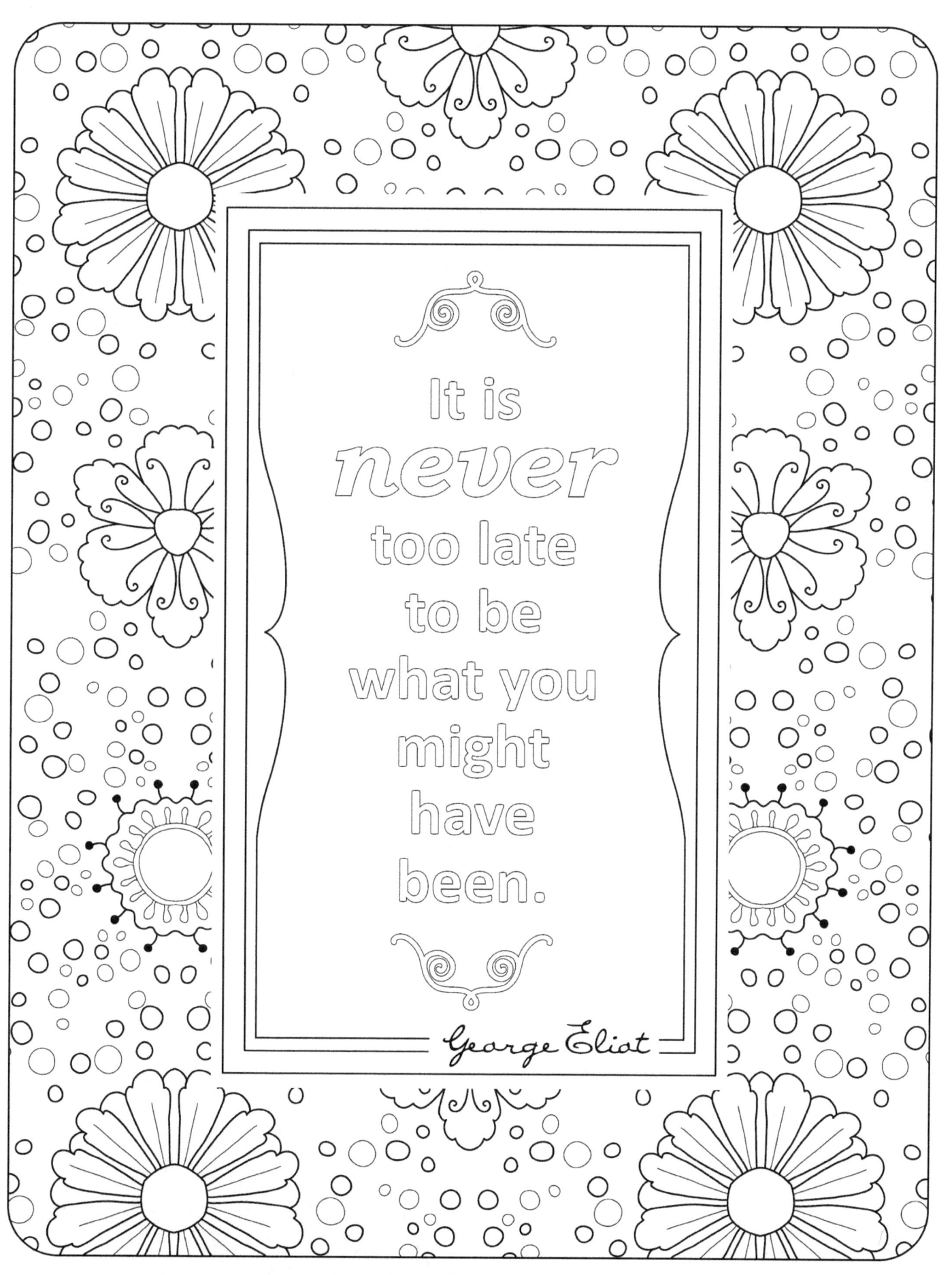

It is
never
too late
to be
what you
might
have
been.

George Eliot

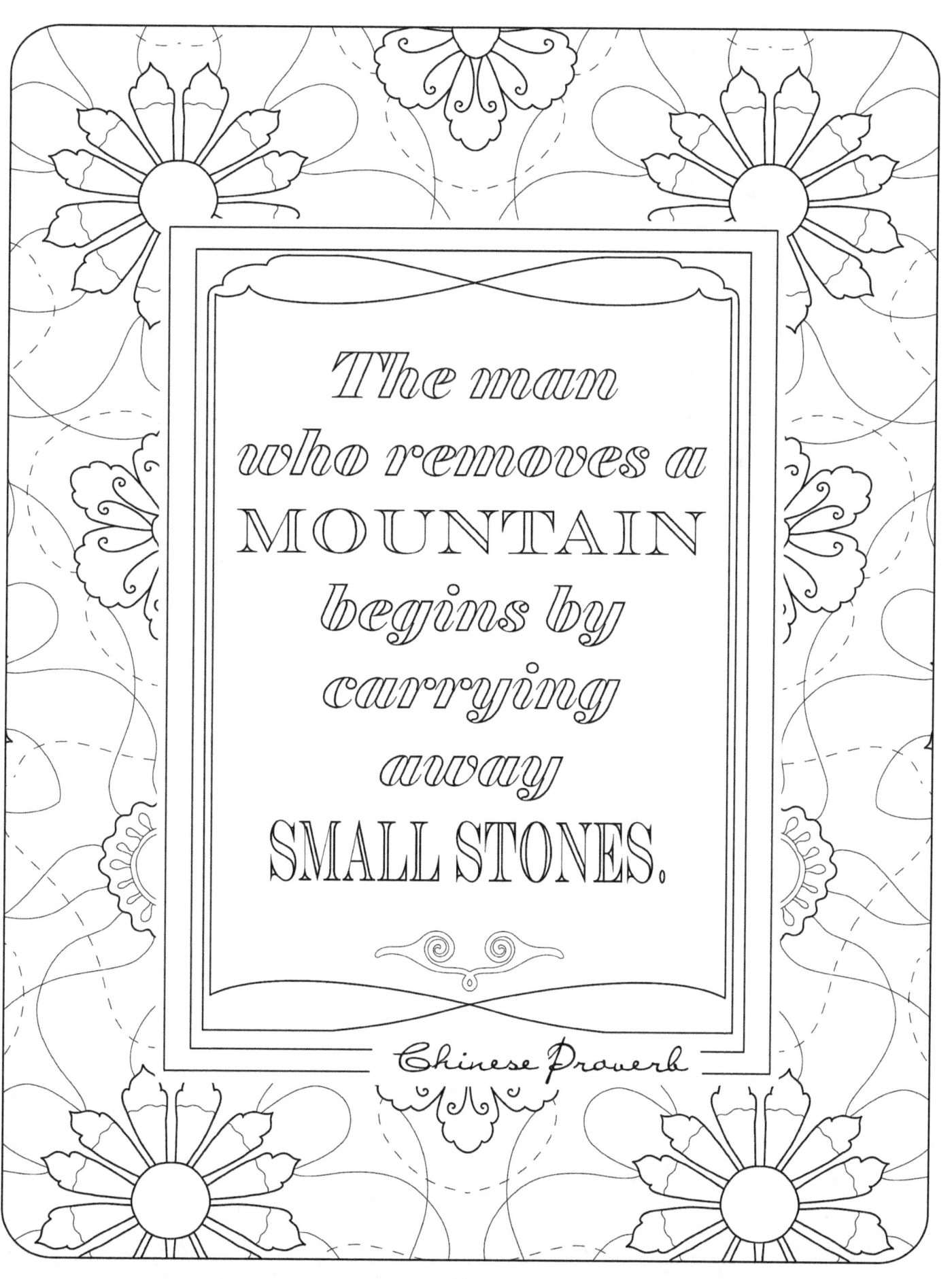

The man
who removes a
MOUNTAIN
begins by
carrying
away
SMALL STONES.

Chinese Proverb

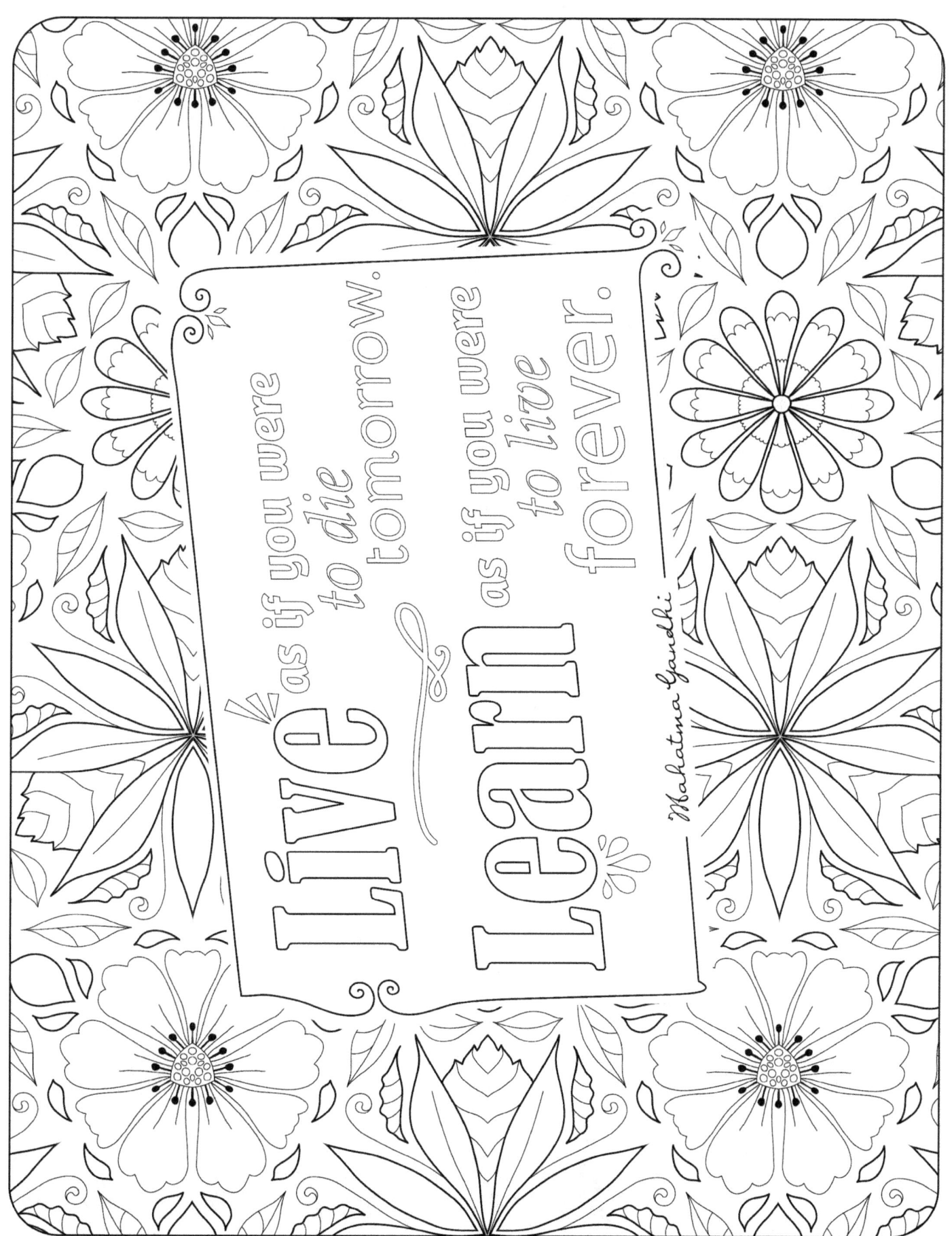

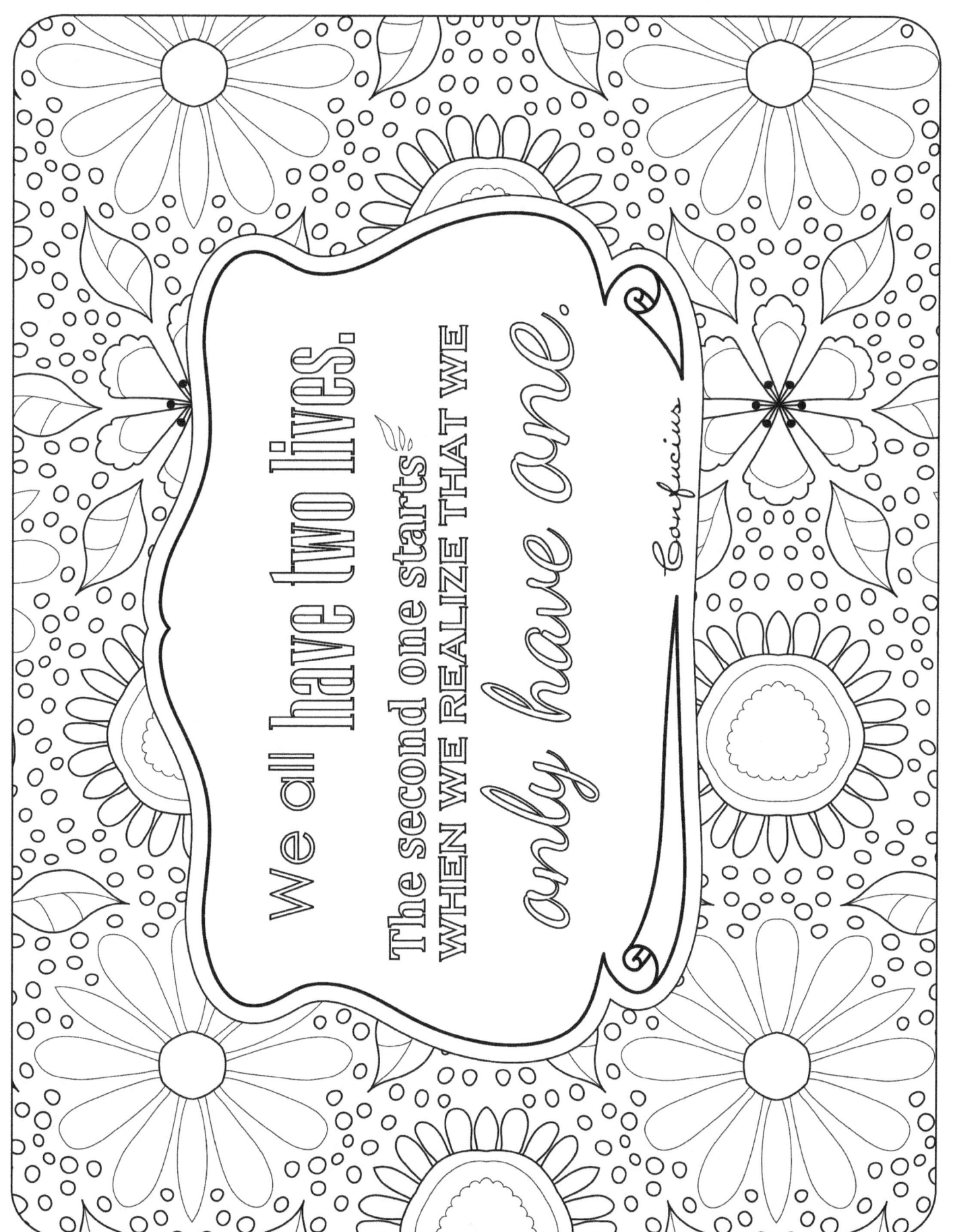

We all have two lives.
The second one starts
WHEN WE REALIZE THAT WE
only have one.

Confucius

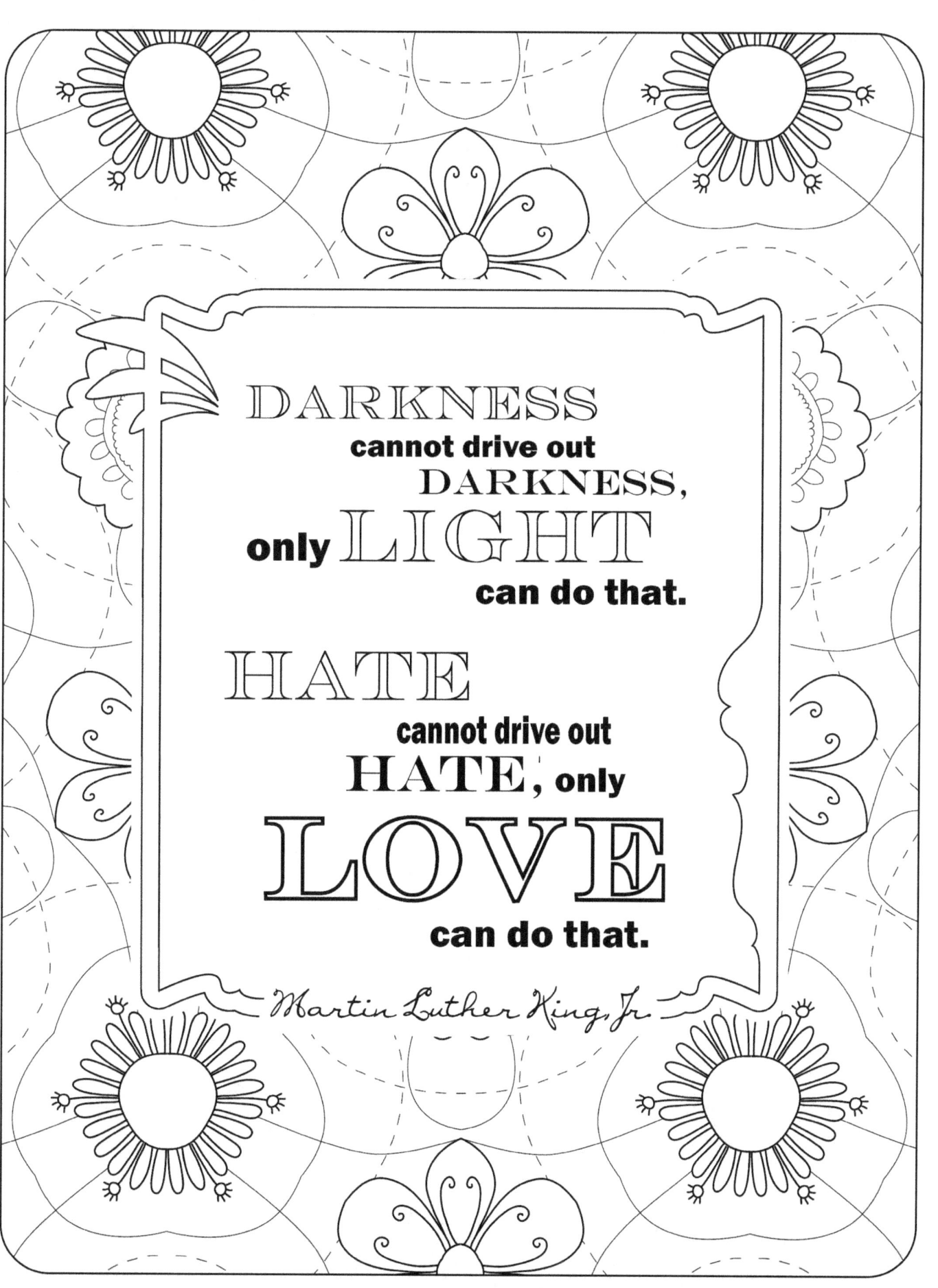

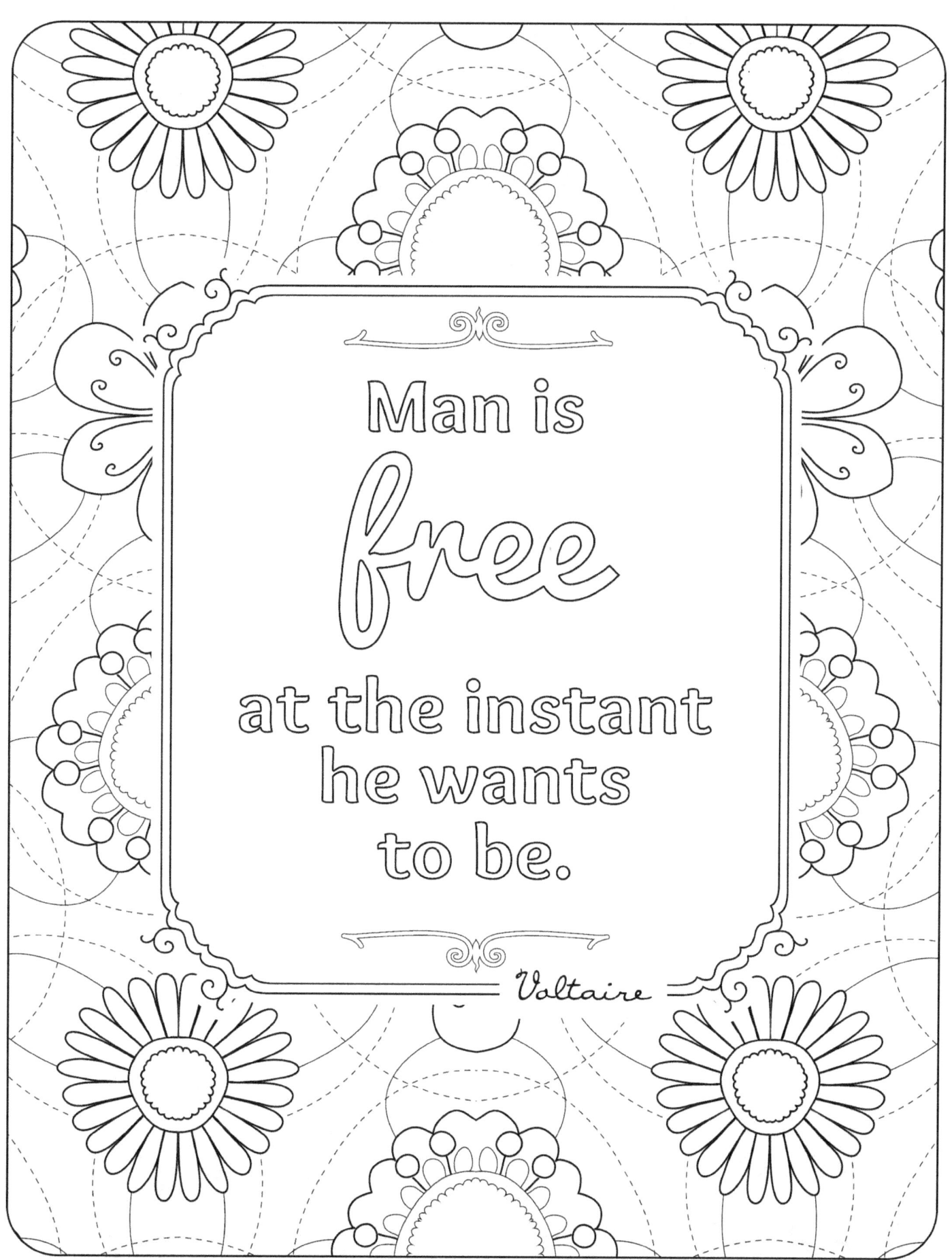

Man is
free
at the instant
he wants
to be.

— Voltaire

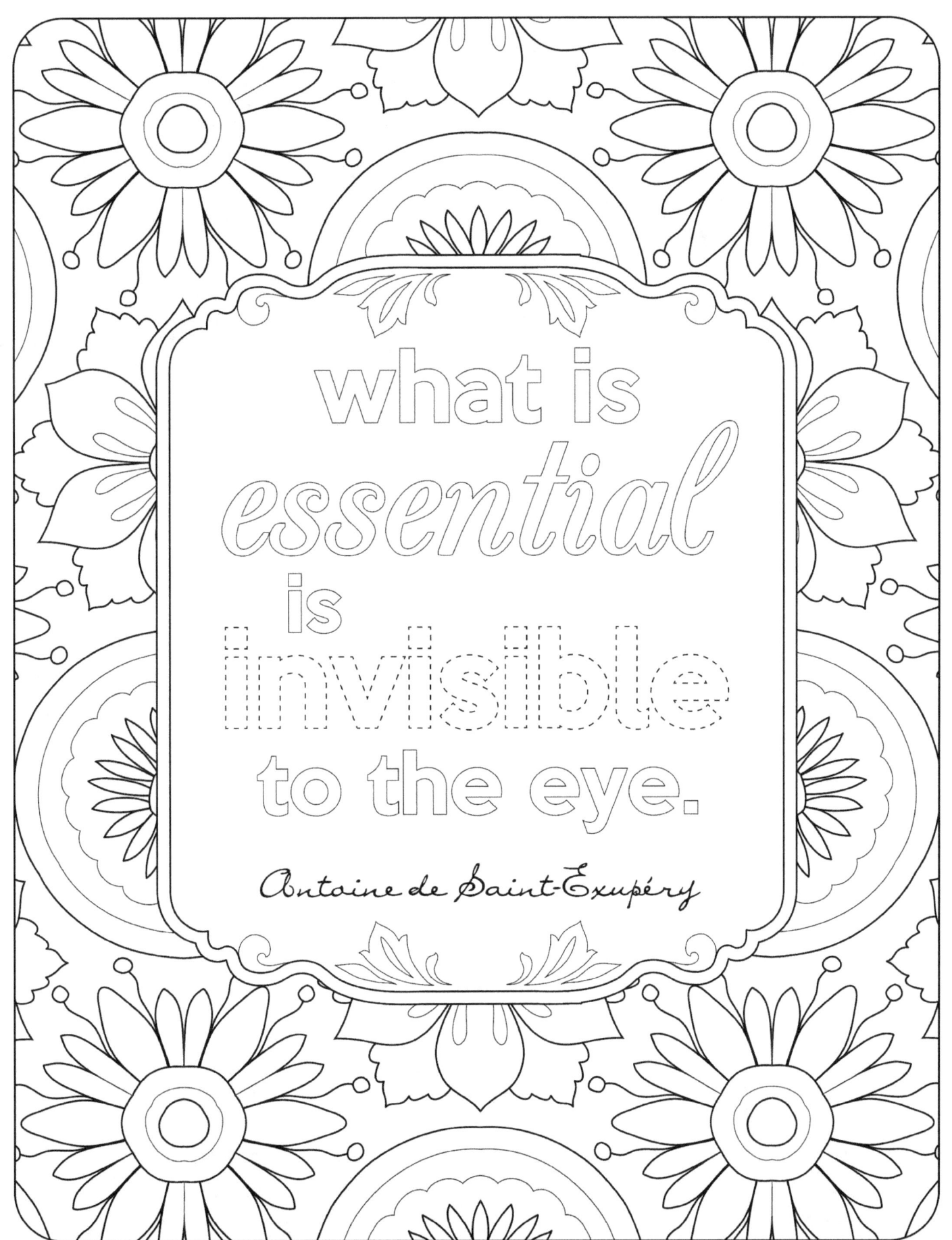

what is *essential* is invisible to the eye.

Antoine de Saint-Exupéry

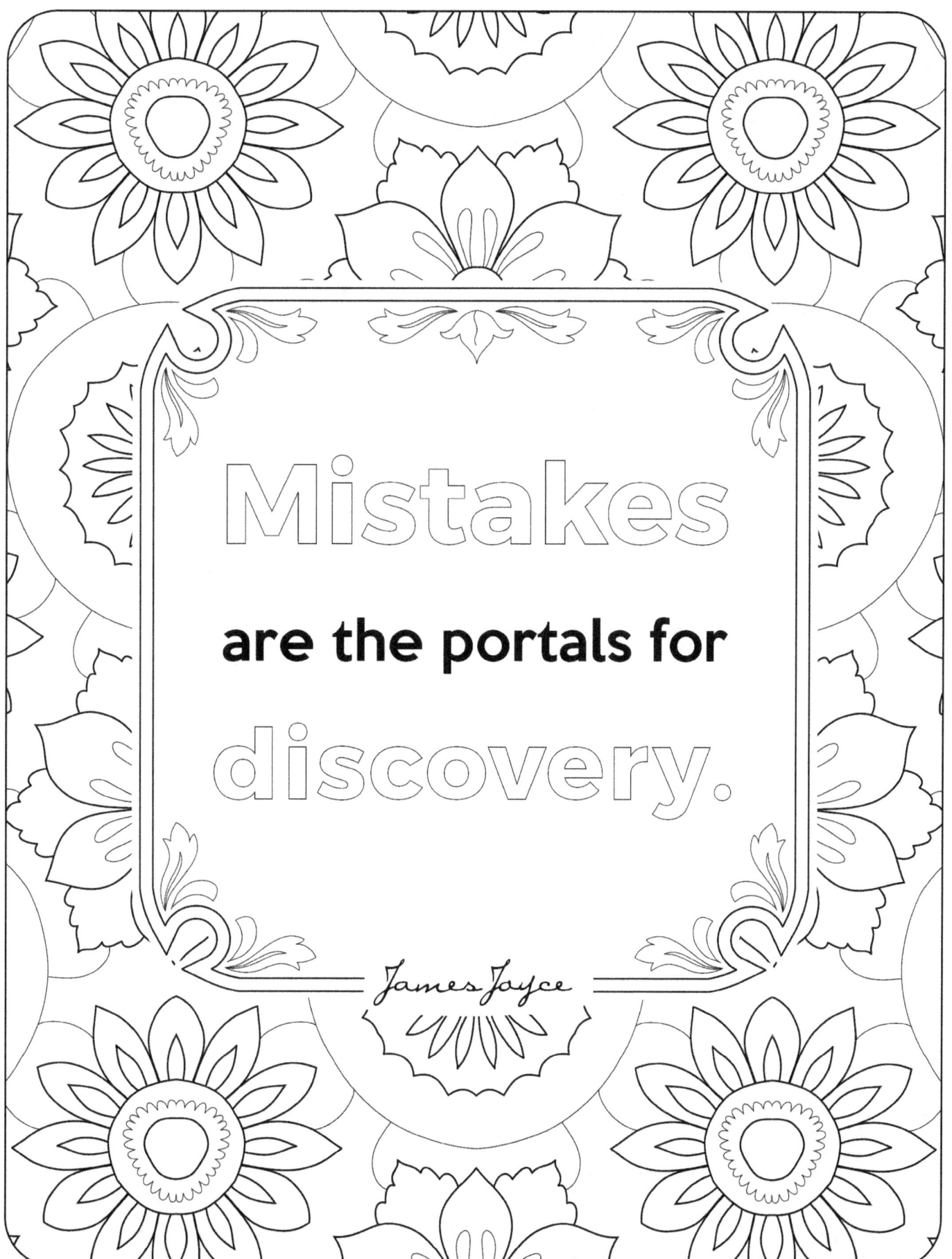

Mistakes

are the portals for

discovery.

James Joyce

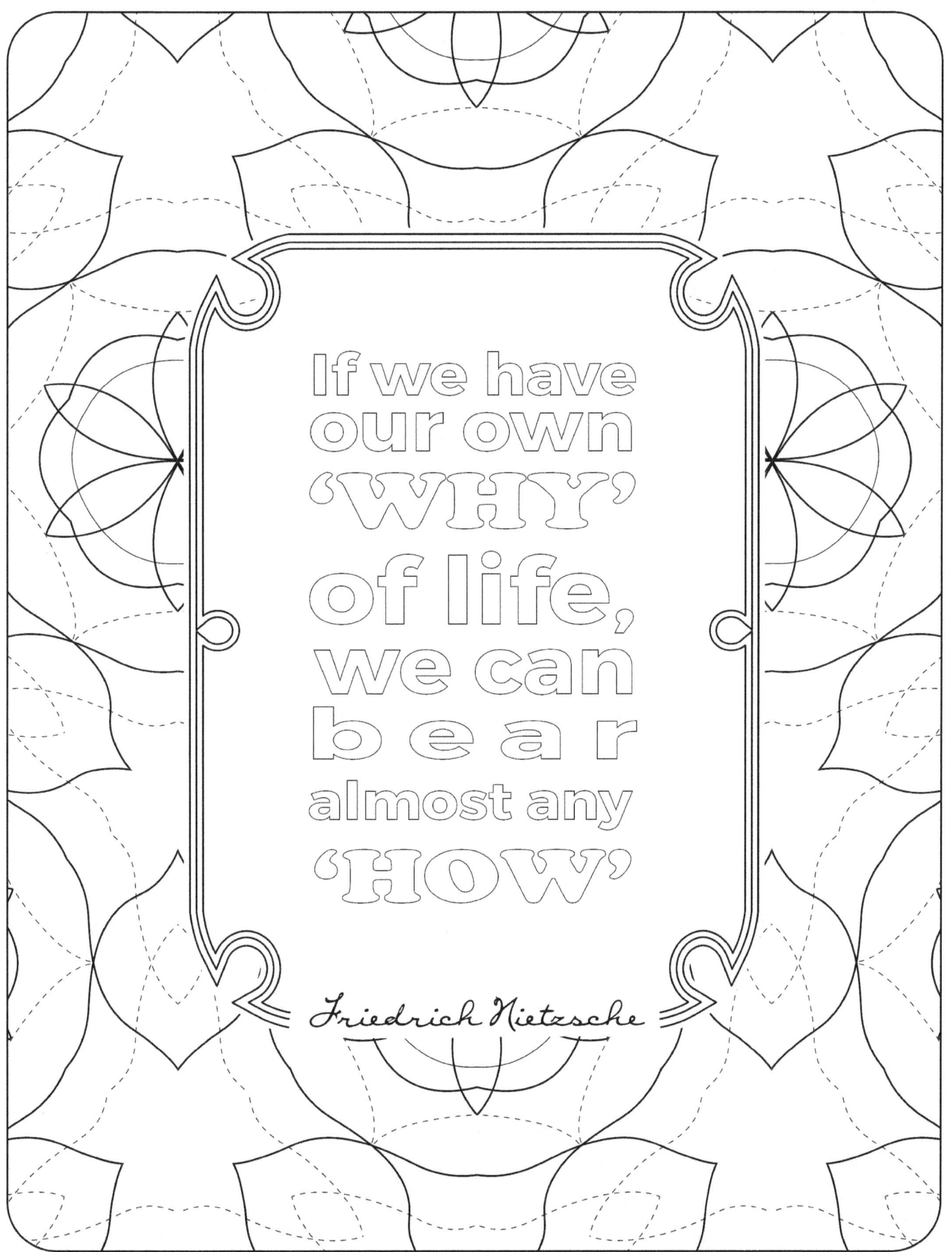

If we have
our own
'WHY'
of life,
we can
b e a r
almost any
'HOW'

Friedrich Nietzsche

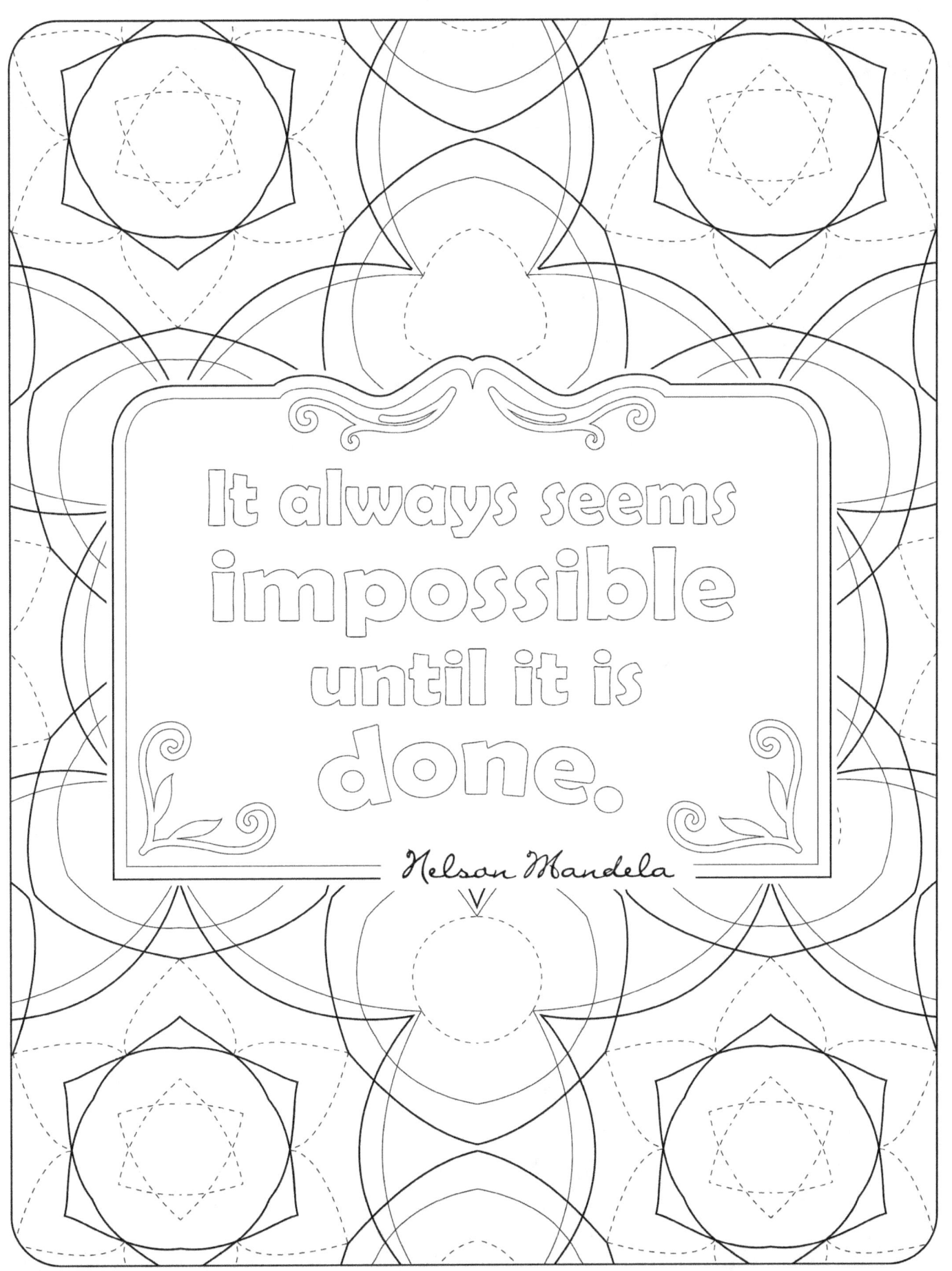

It always seems impossible until it is done.

Nelson Mandela

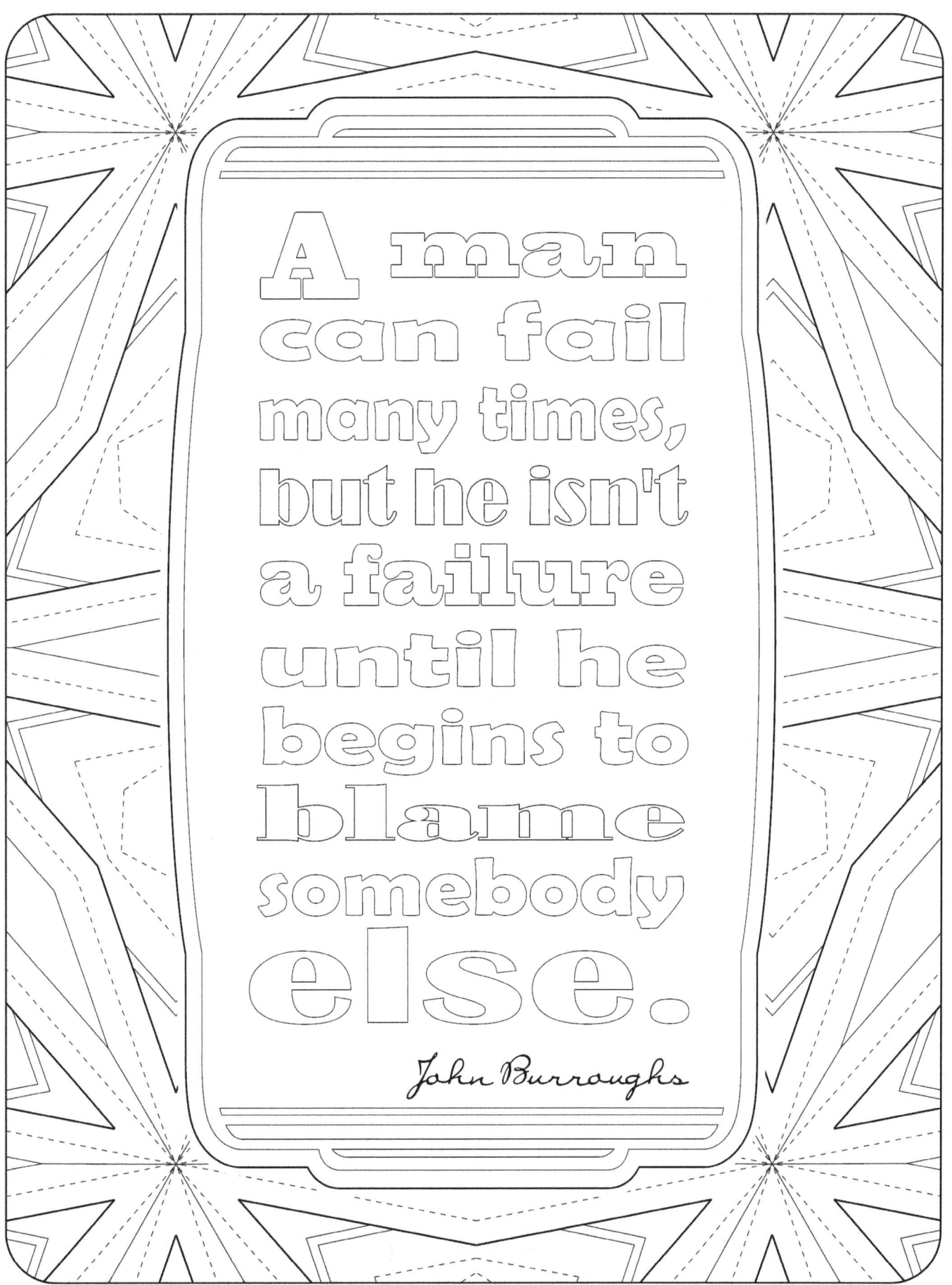

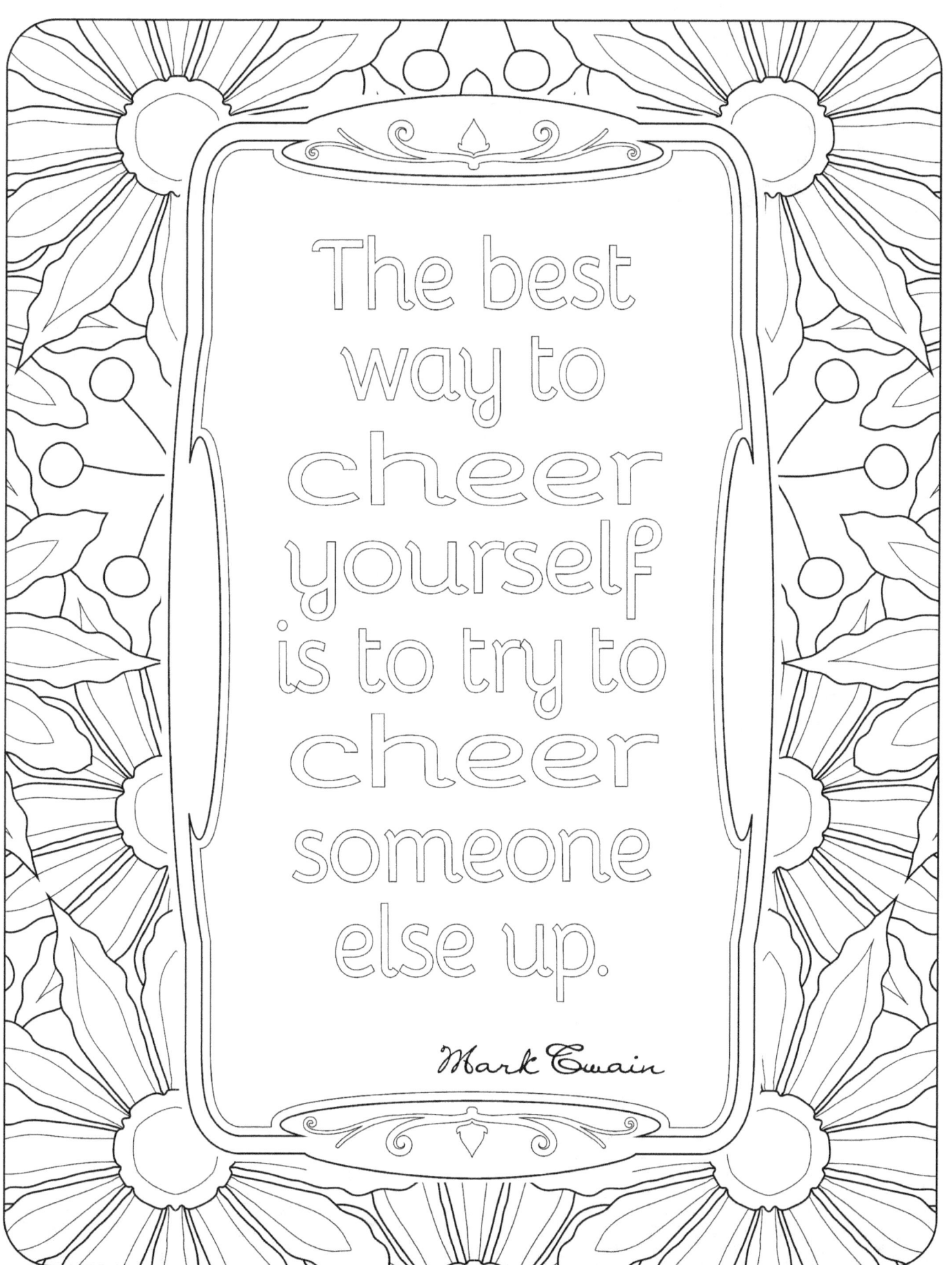

The best way to cheer yourself is to try to cheer someone else up.

Mark Twain

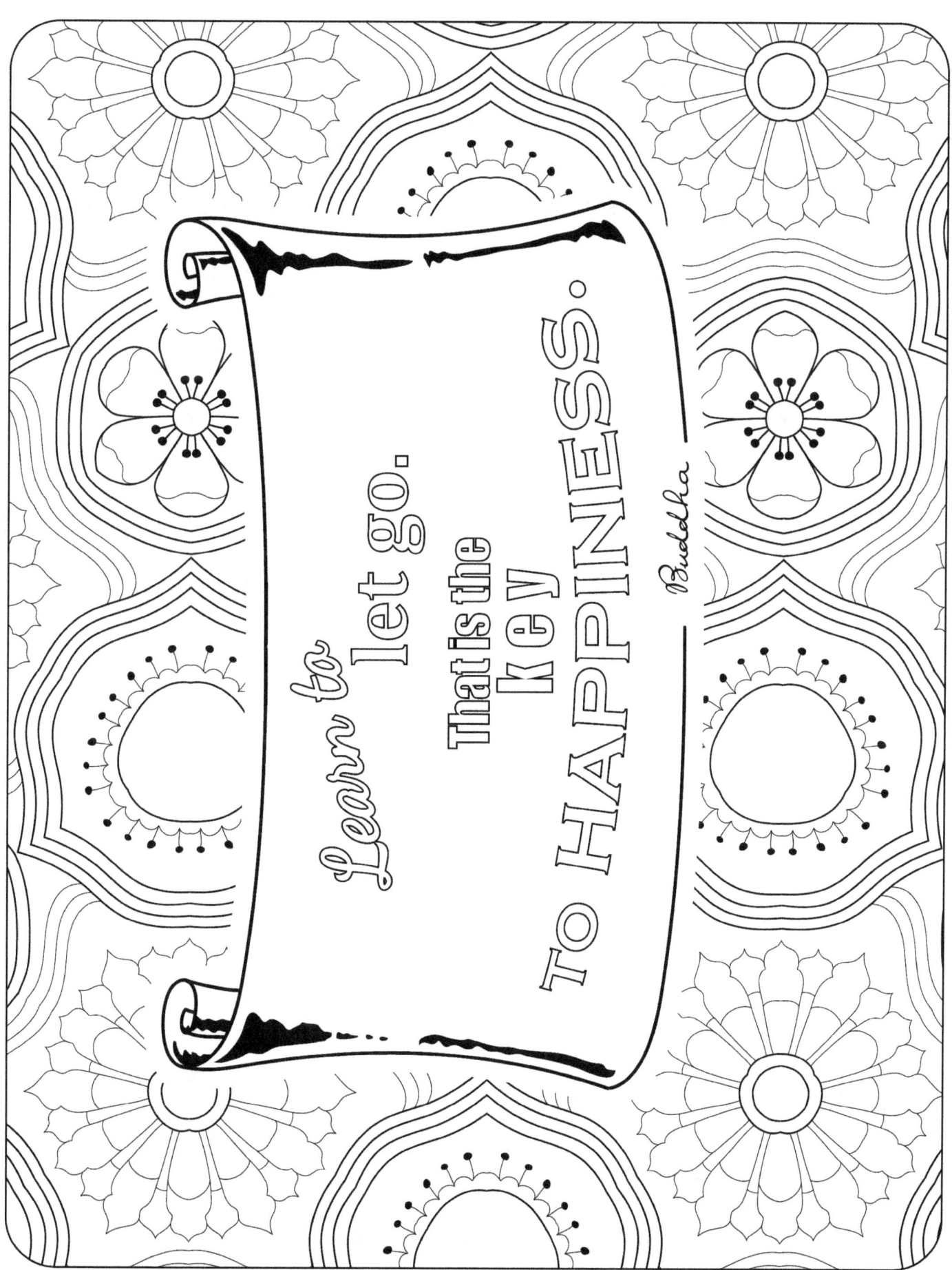

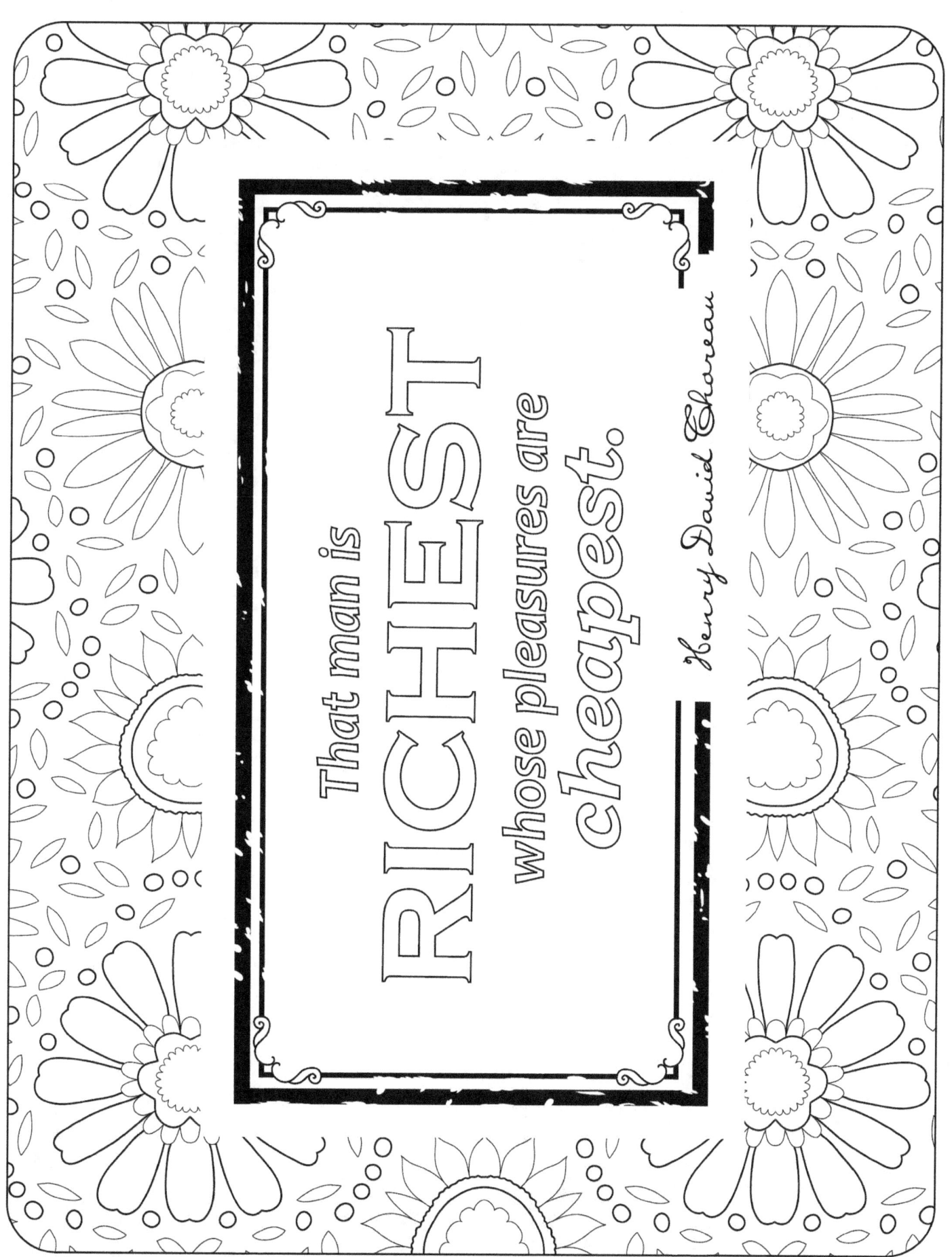

That man is RICHEST whose pleasures are cheapest.

Henry David Thoreau

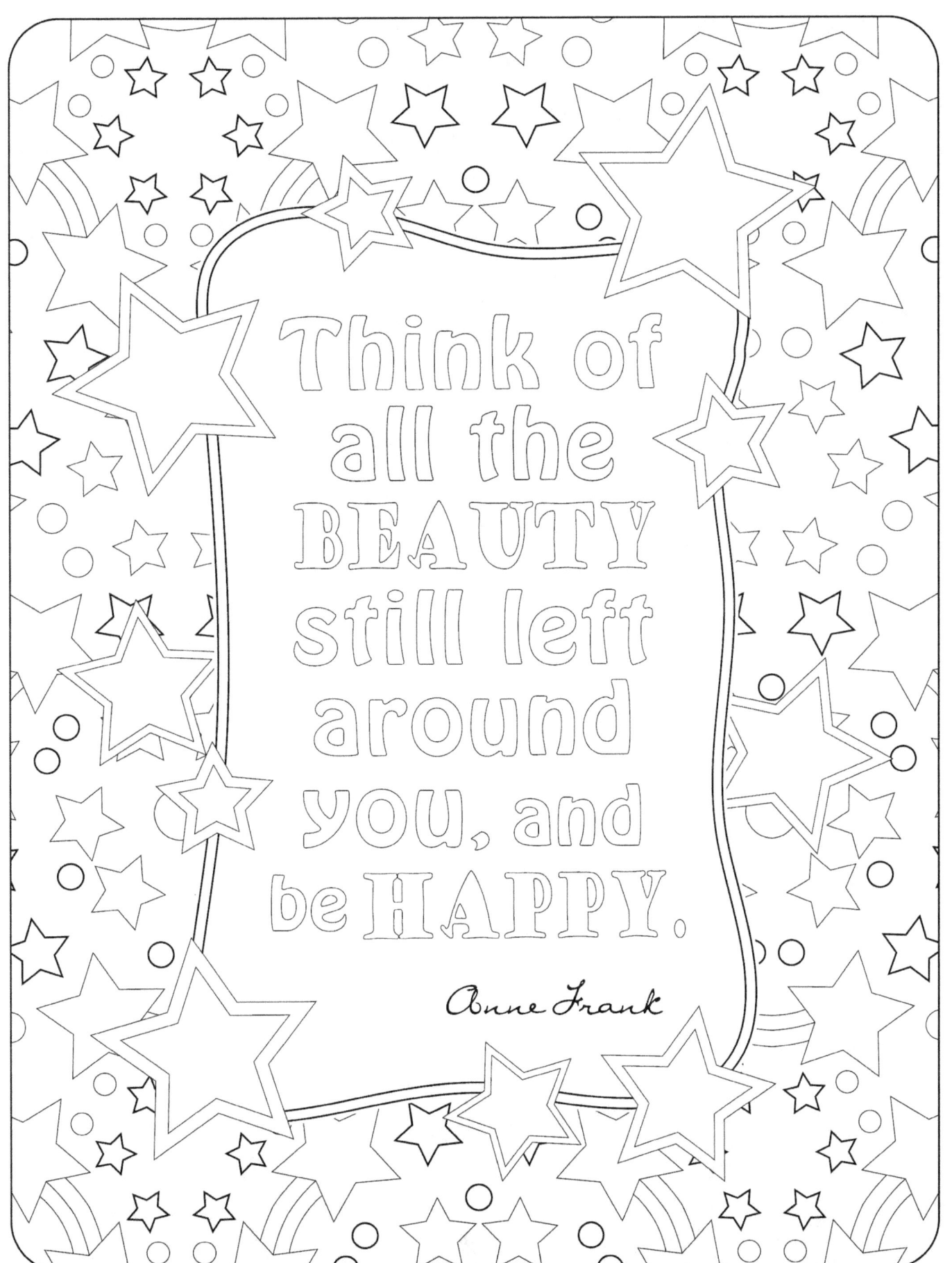

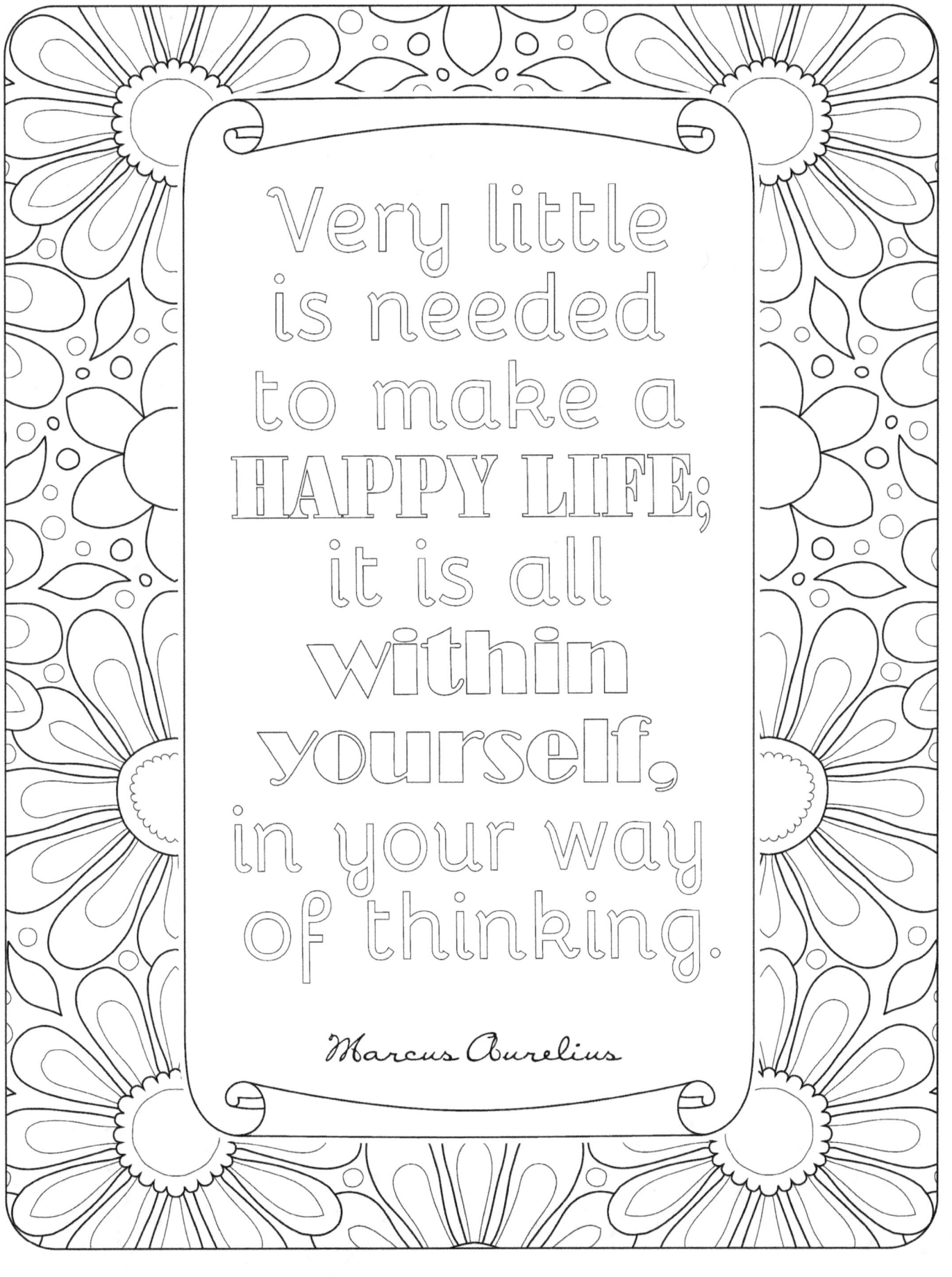

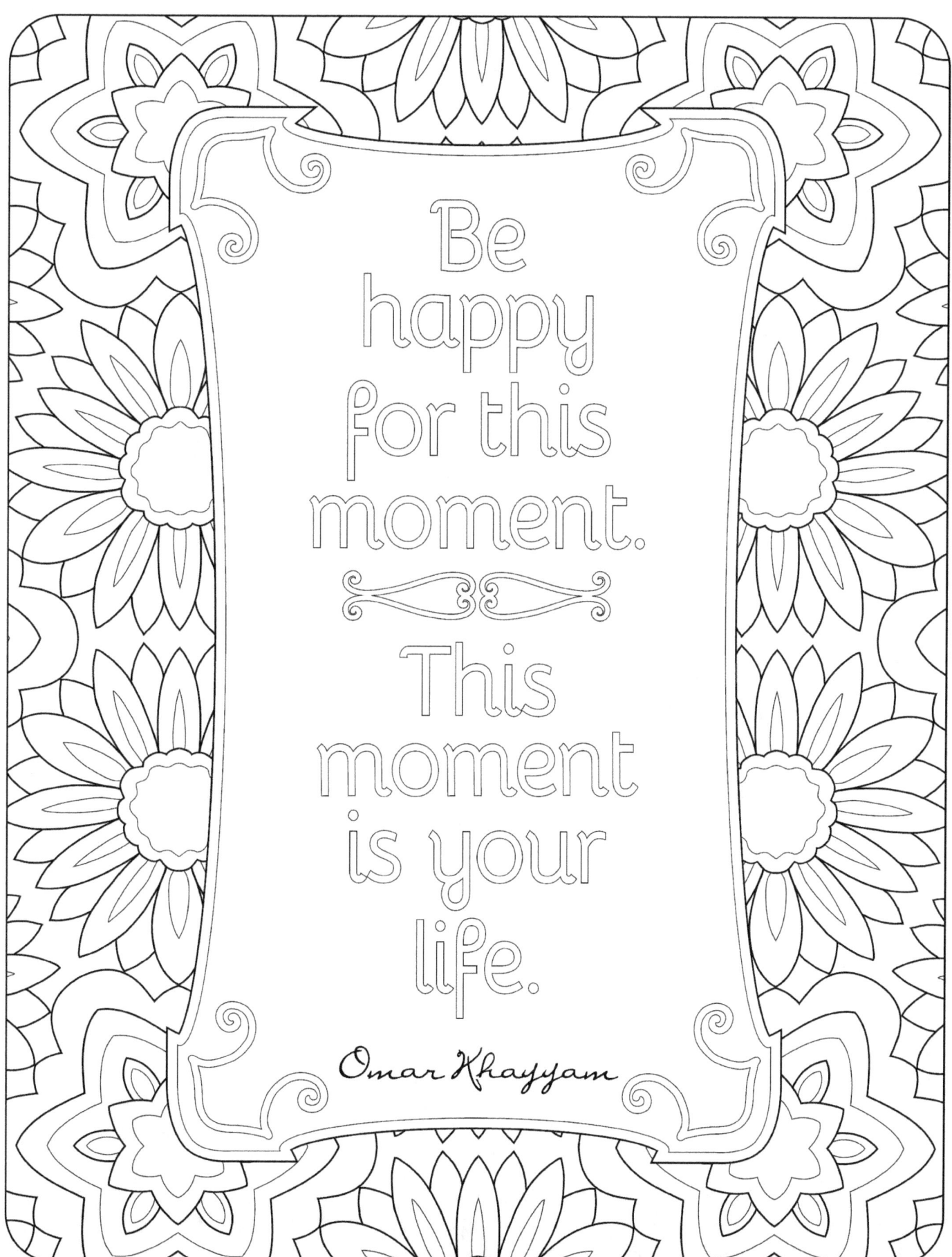

Be happy for this moment. This moment is your life.

Omar Khayyam

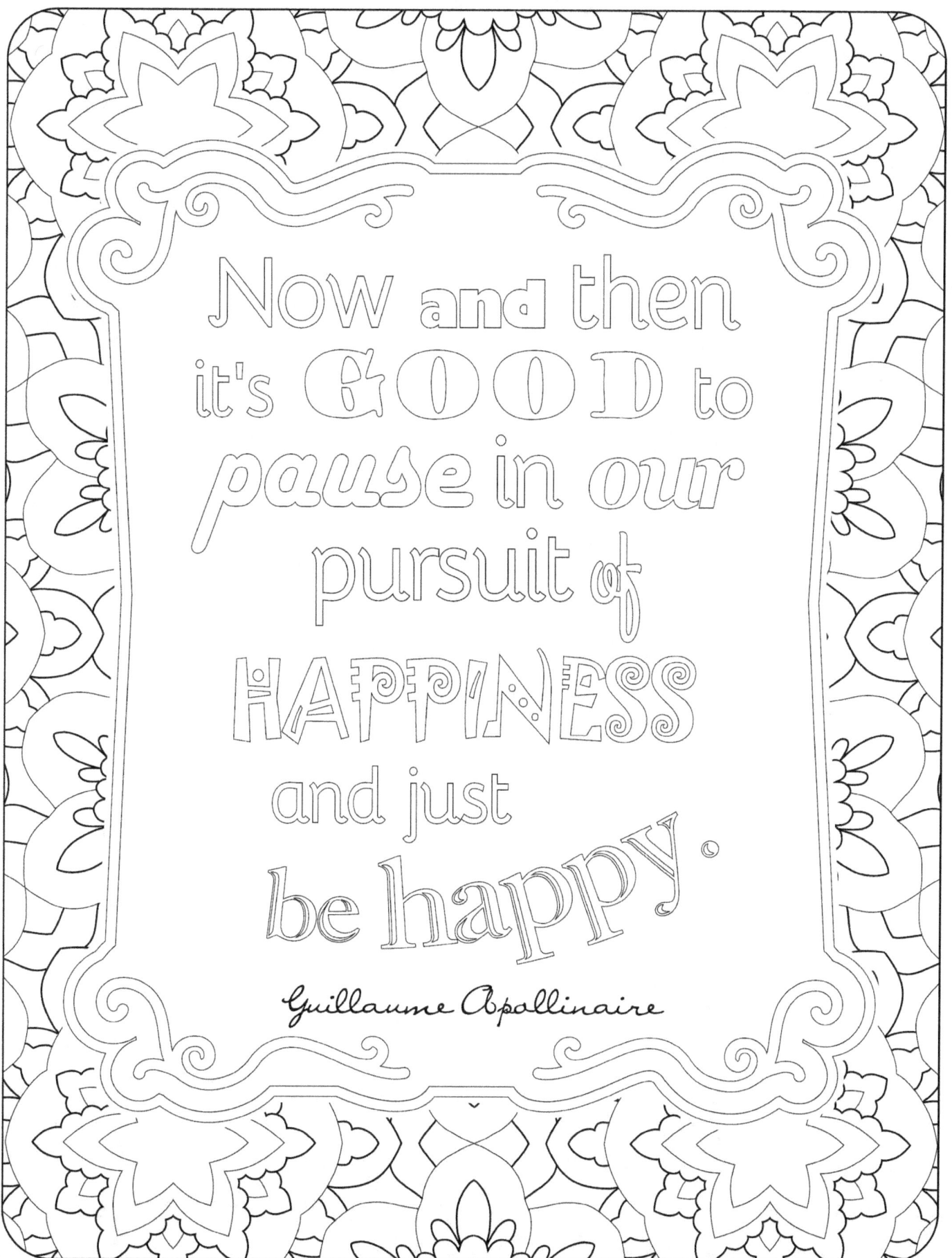

Now and then it's GOOD to pause in our pursuit of HAPPINESS and just be happy.

Guillaume Apollinaire

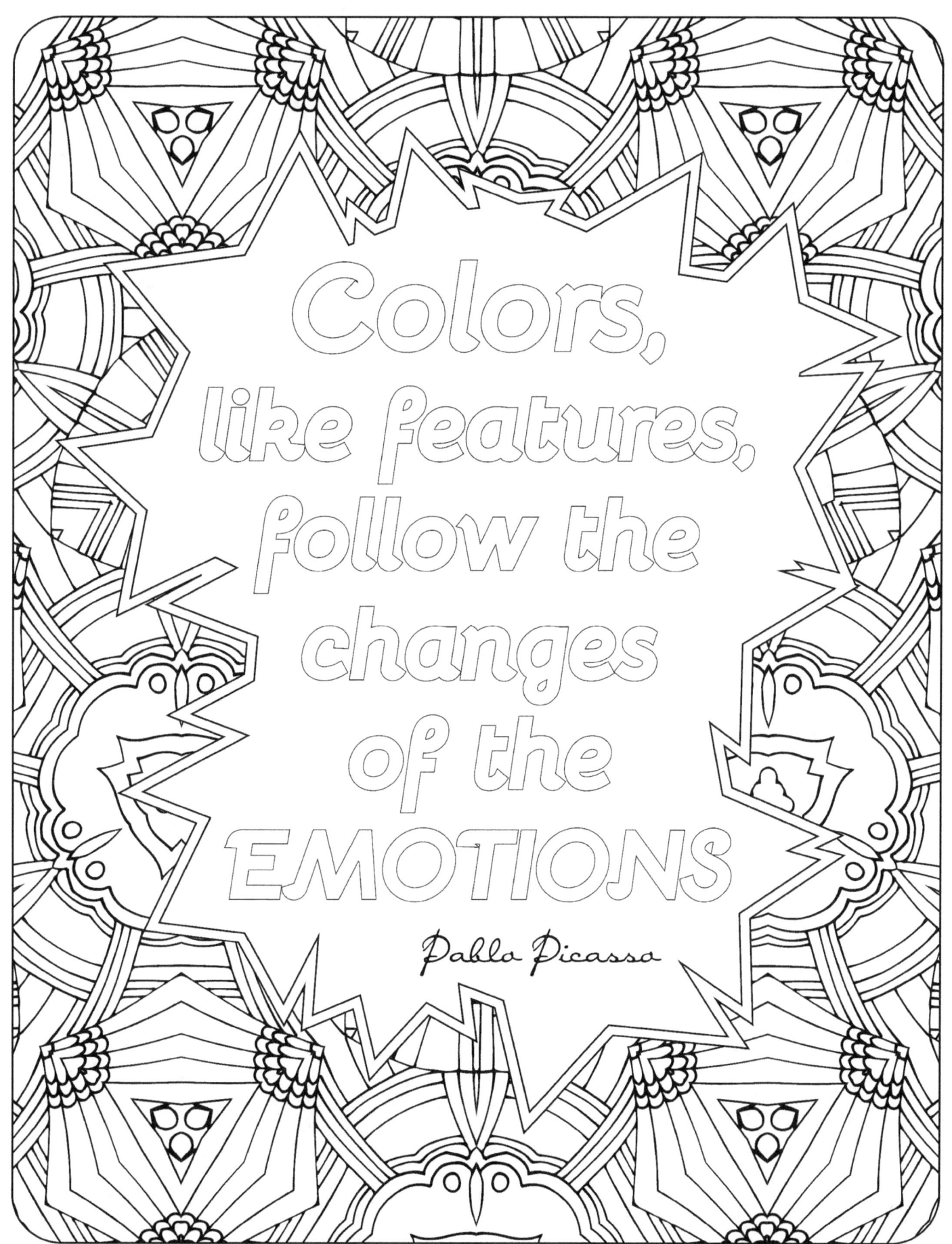

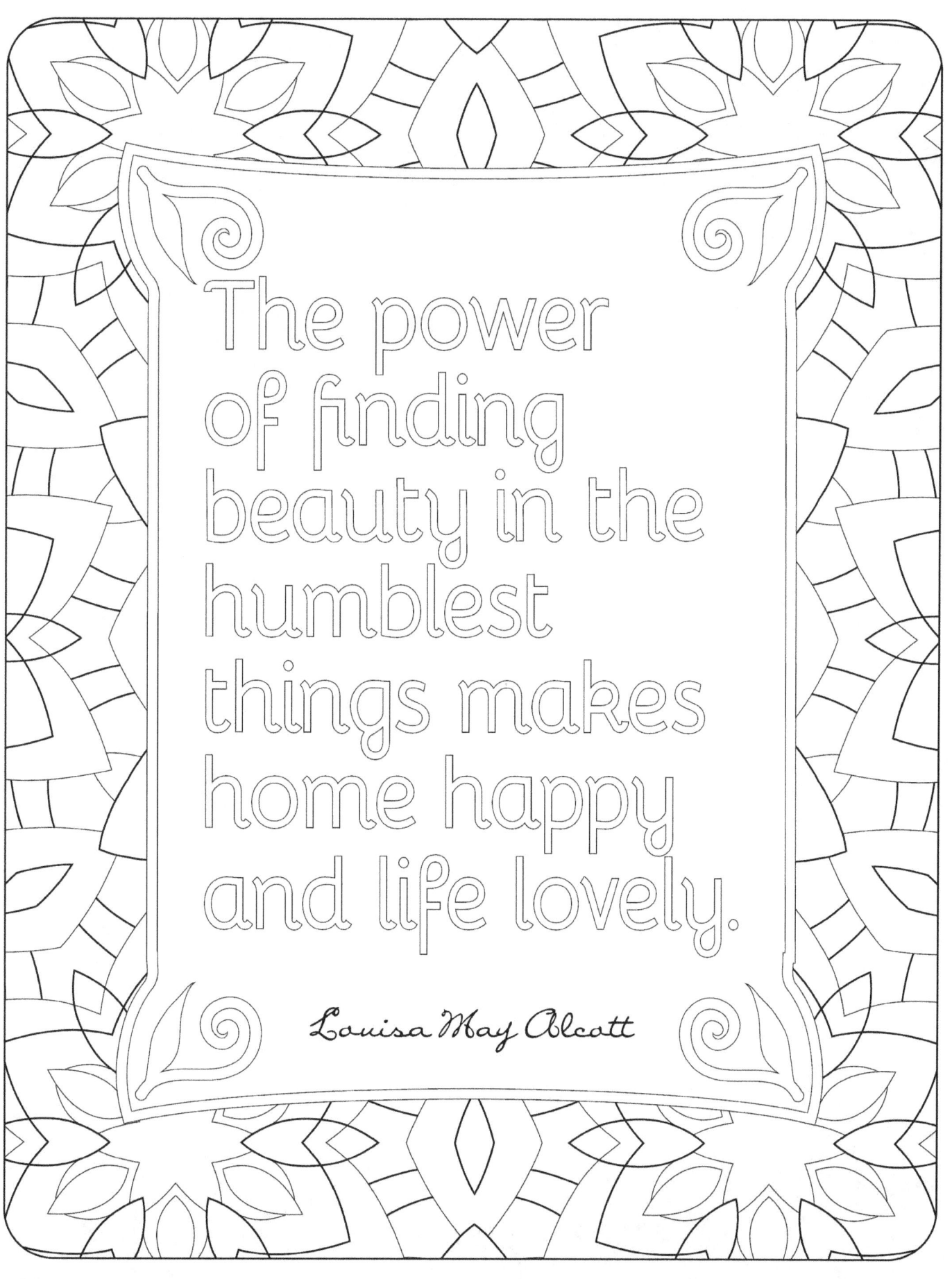

The power of finding beauty in the humblest things makes home happy and life lovely.

Louisa May Alcott

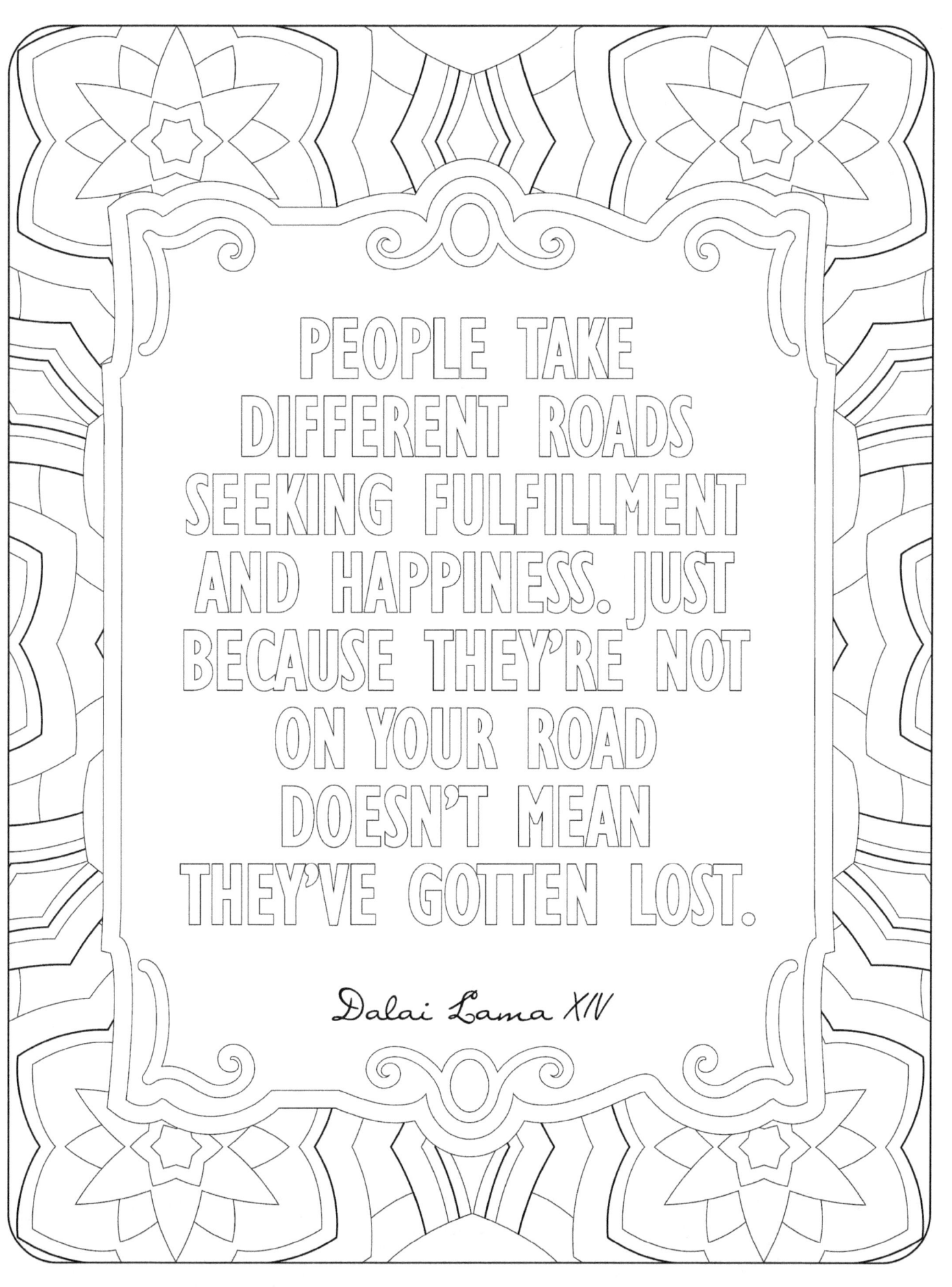

PEOPLE TAKE
DIFFERENT ROADS
SEEKING FULFILLMENT
AND HAPPINESS. JUST
BECAUSE THEY'RE NOT
ON YOUR ROAD
DOESN'T MEAN
THEY'VE GOTTEN LOST.

Dalai Lama XIV

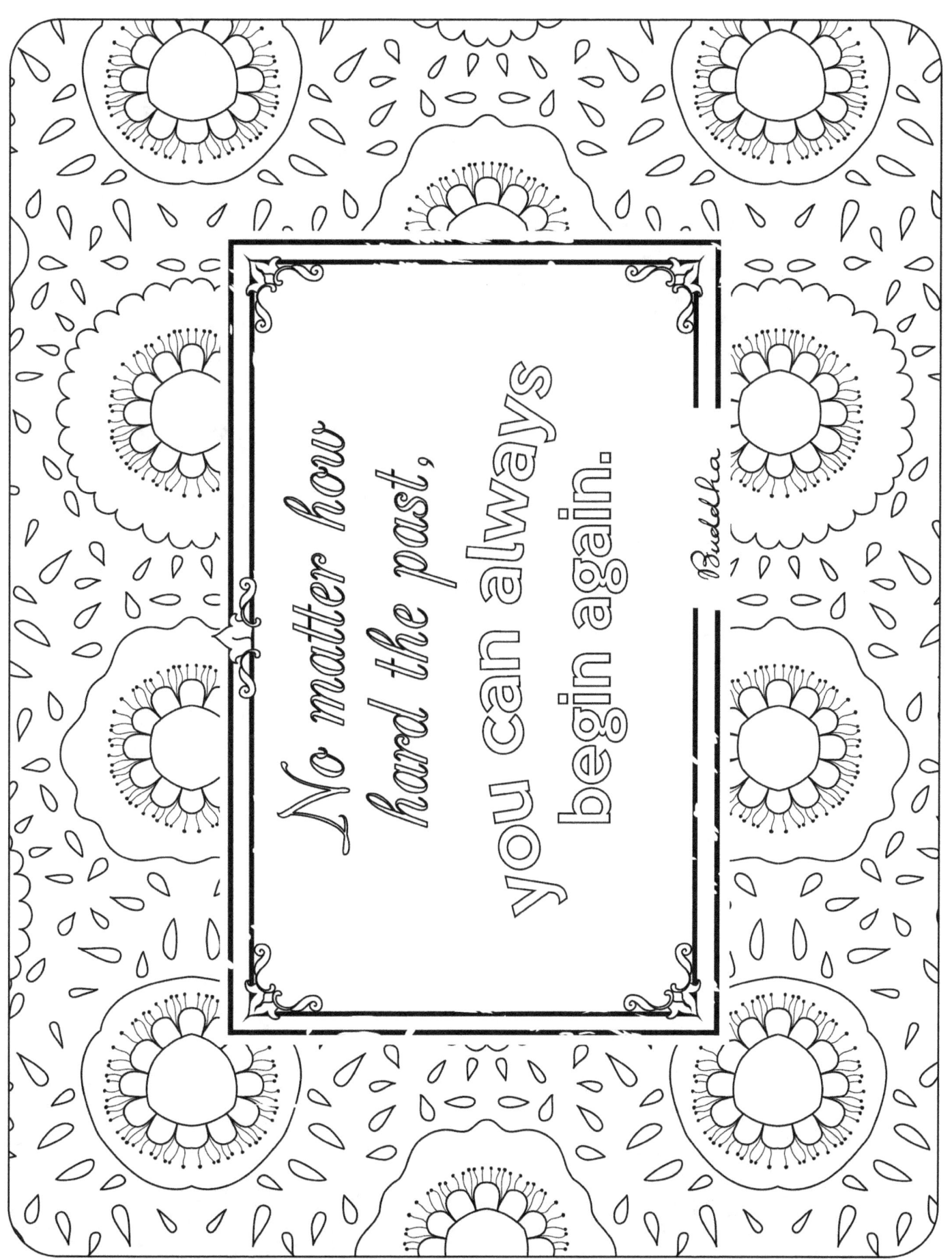

No matter how hard the past, you can always begin again.

Buddha

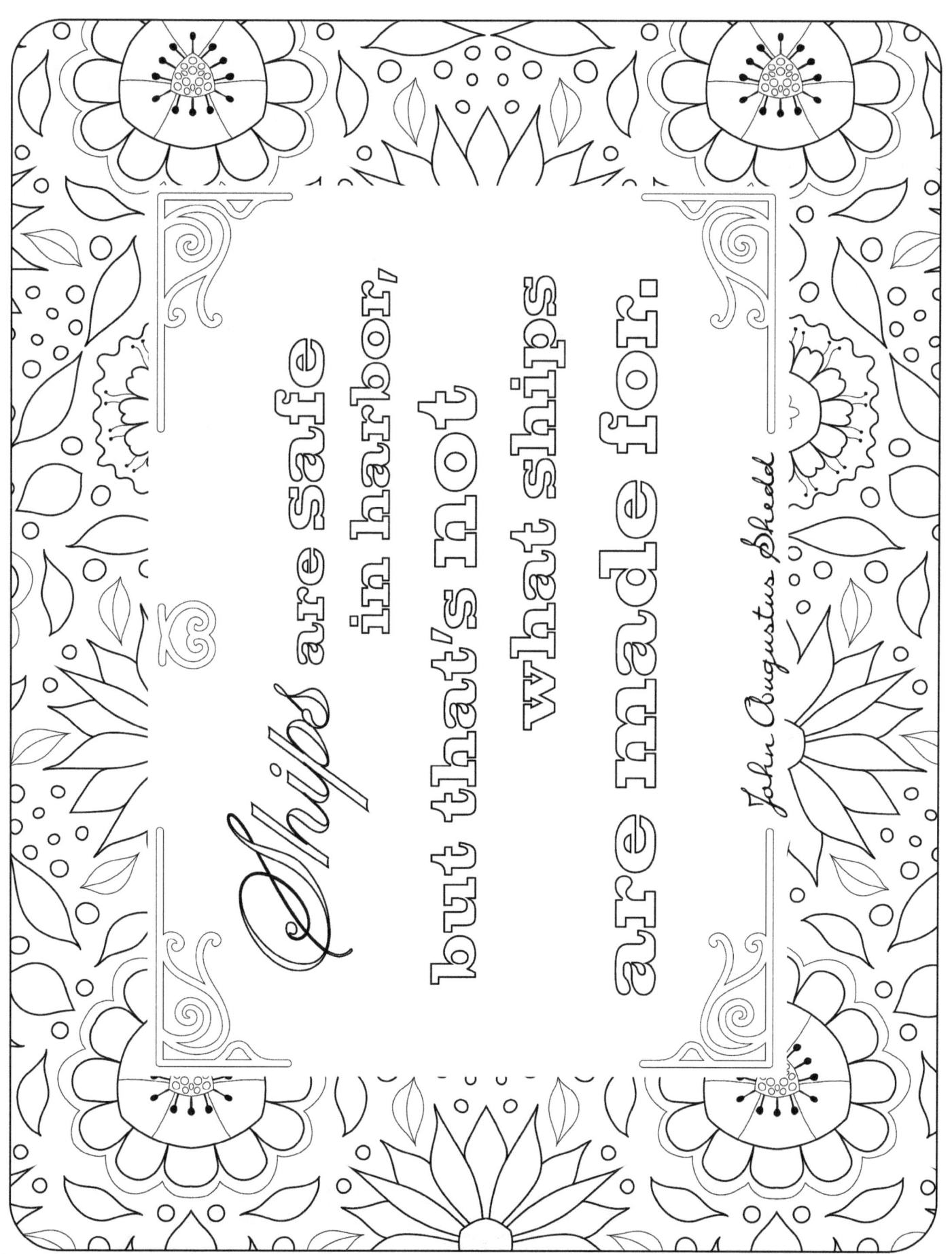

Ships are safe
in harbor,
but that's not
what ships
are made for.

John Augustus Shedd

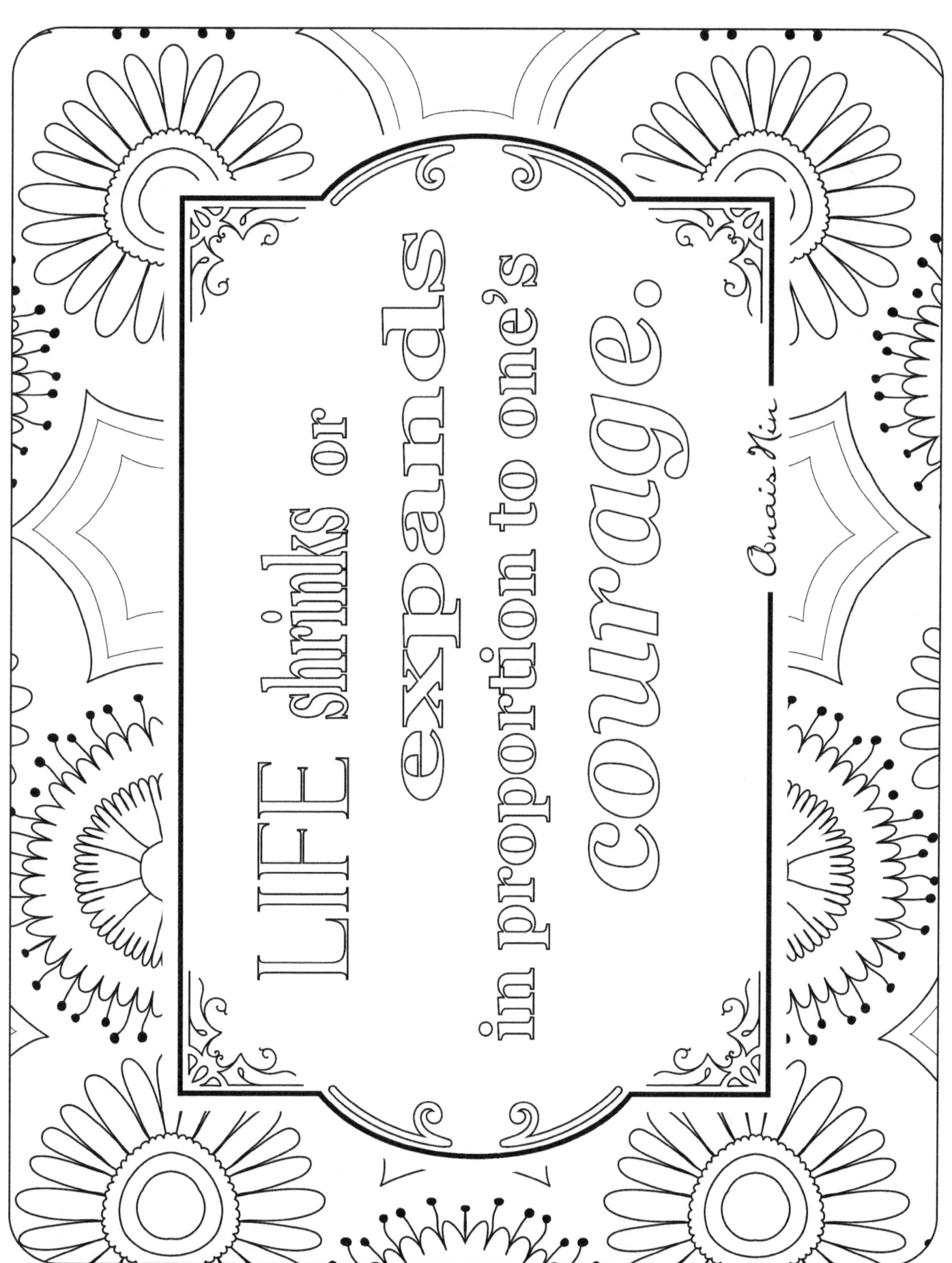

LIFE shrinks or expands in proportion to one's courage.

Anais Nin

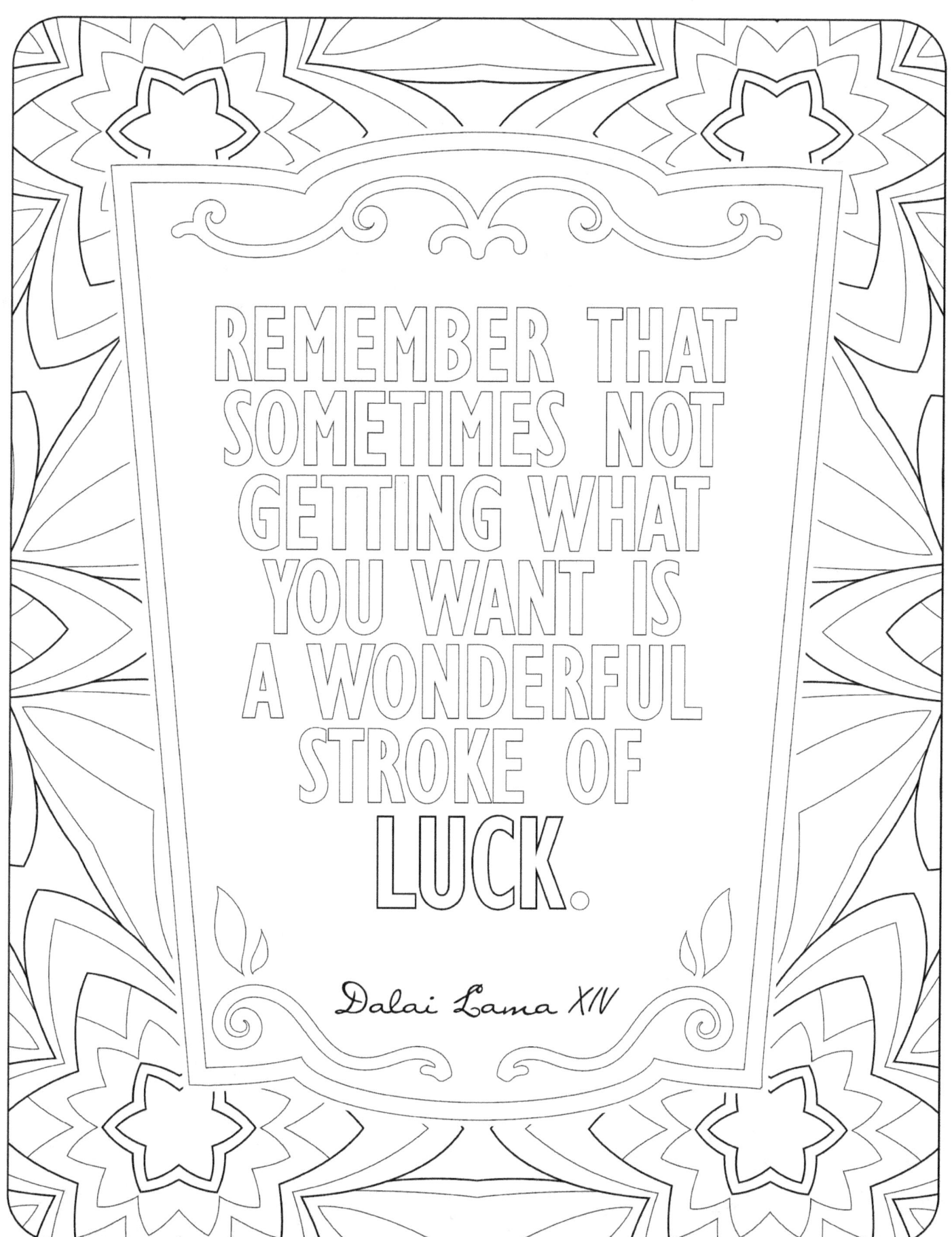

REMEMBER THAT SOMETIMES NOT GETTING WHAT YOU WANT IS A WONDERFUL STROKE OF LUCK.

Dalai Lama XIV

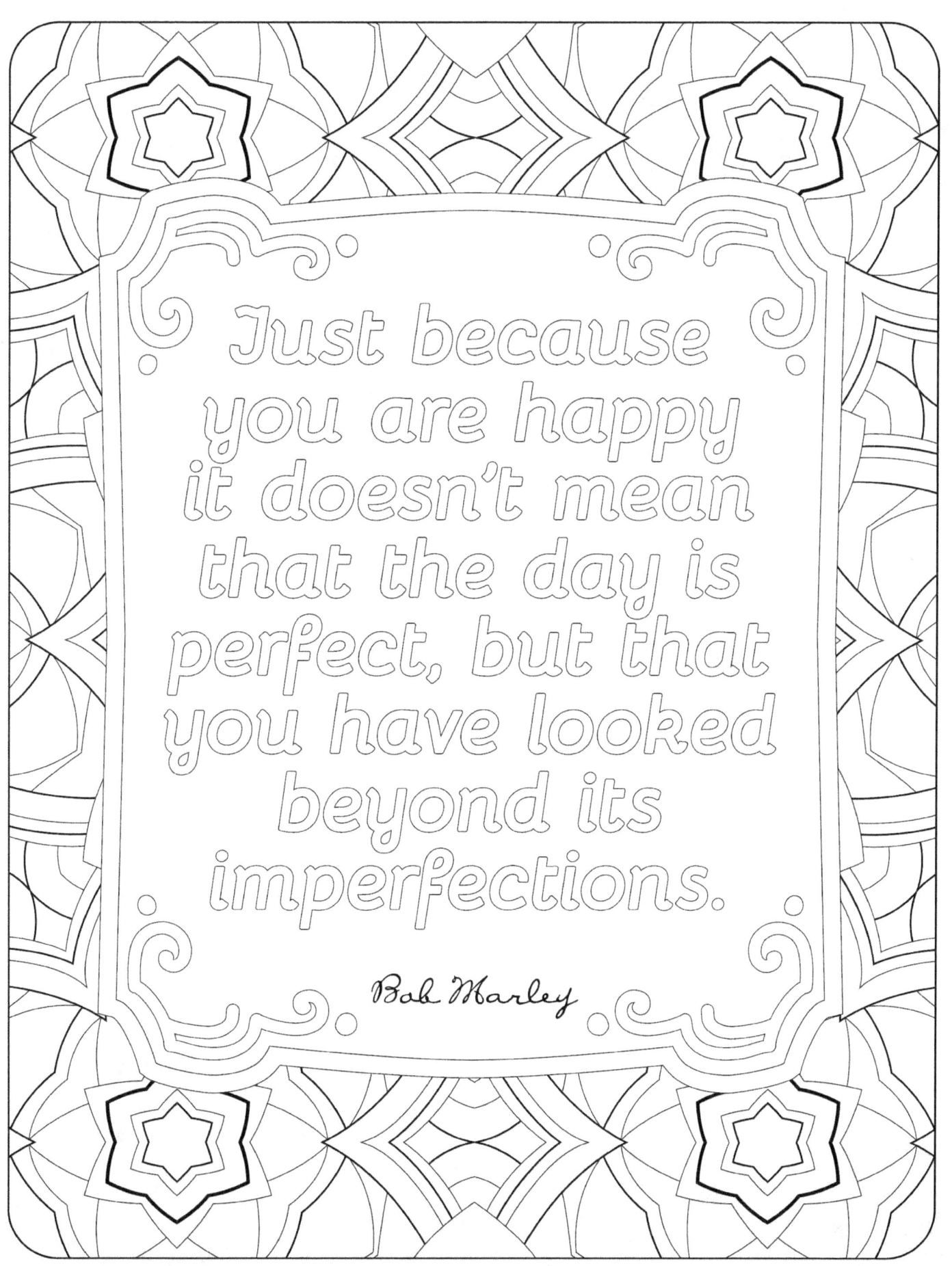

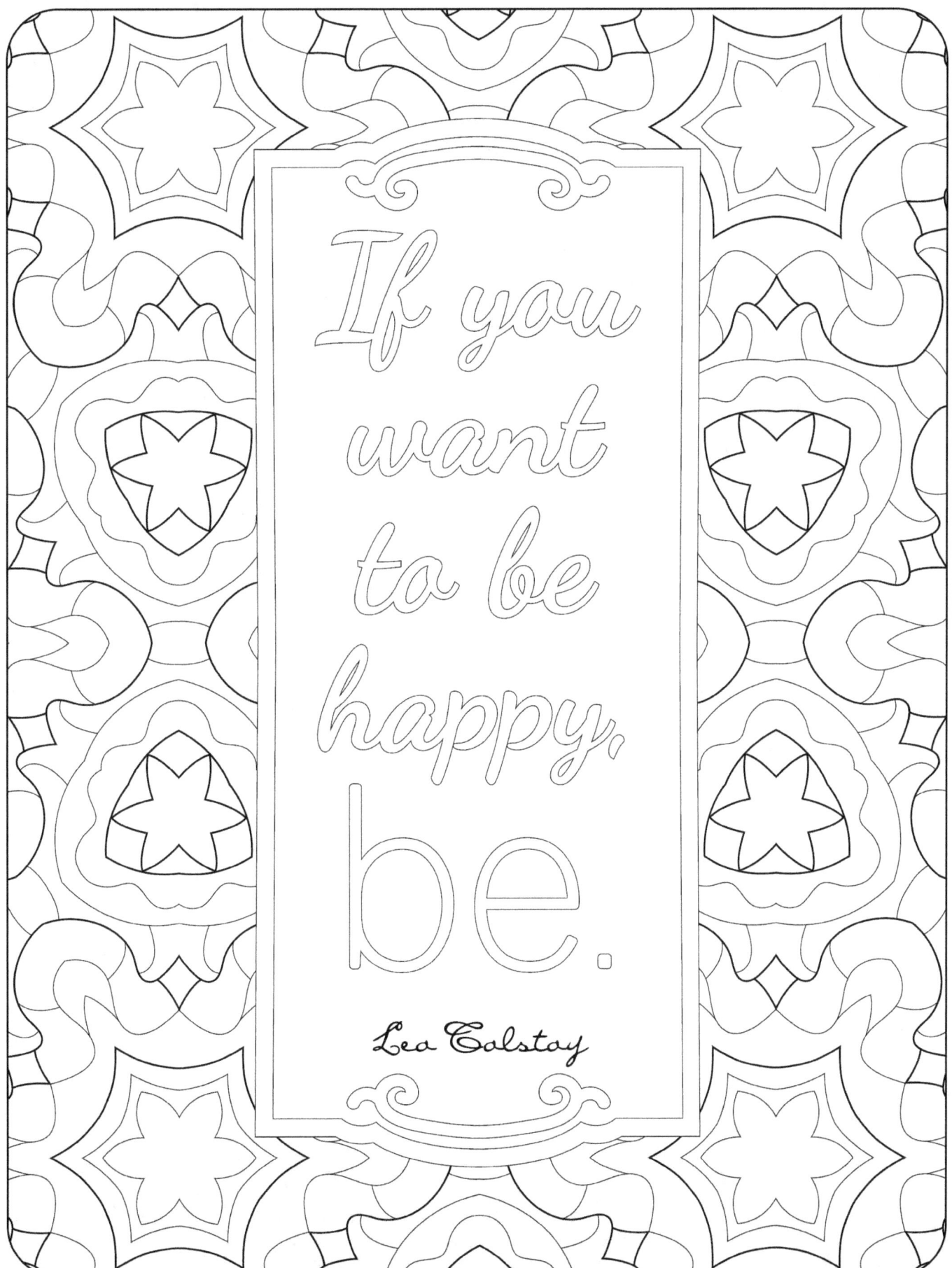

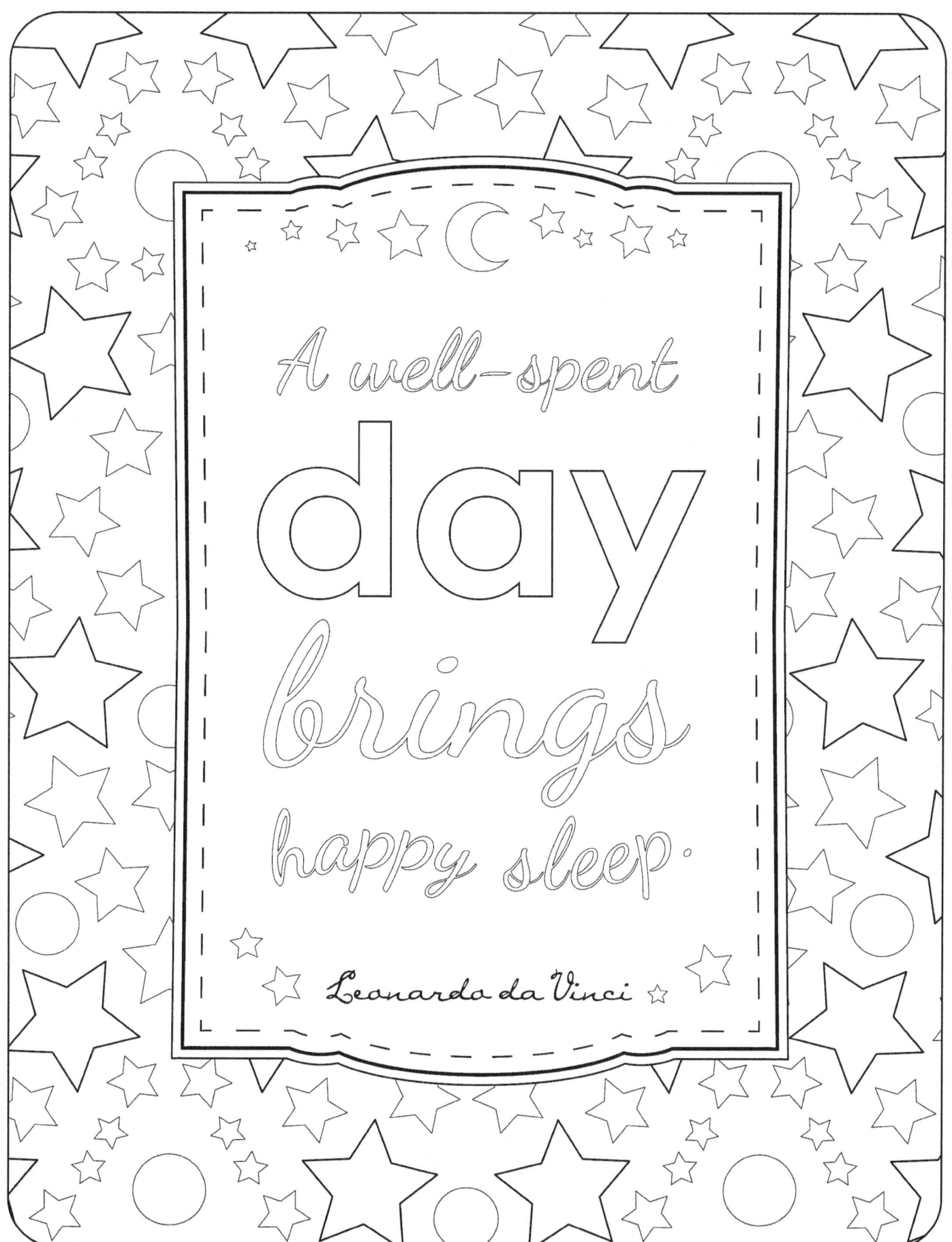

A well-spent day brings happy sleep.

Leonardo da Vinci

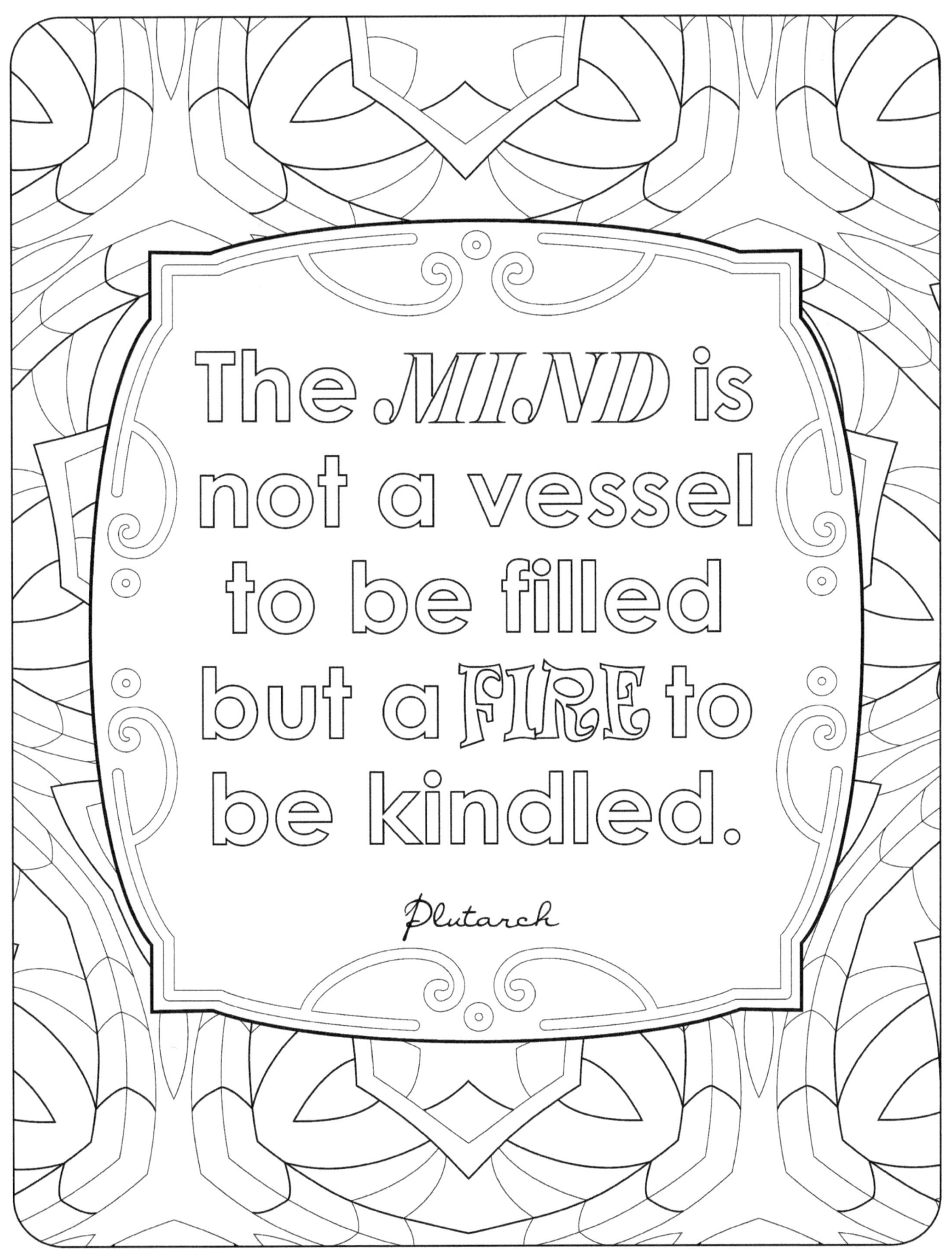

The *MIND* is not a vessel to be filled but a FIRE to be kindled.

Plutarch

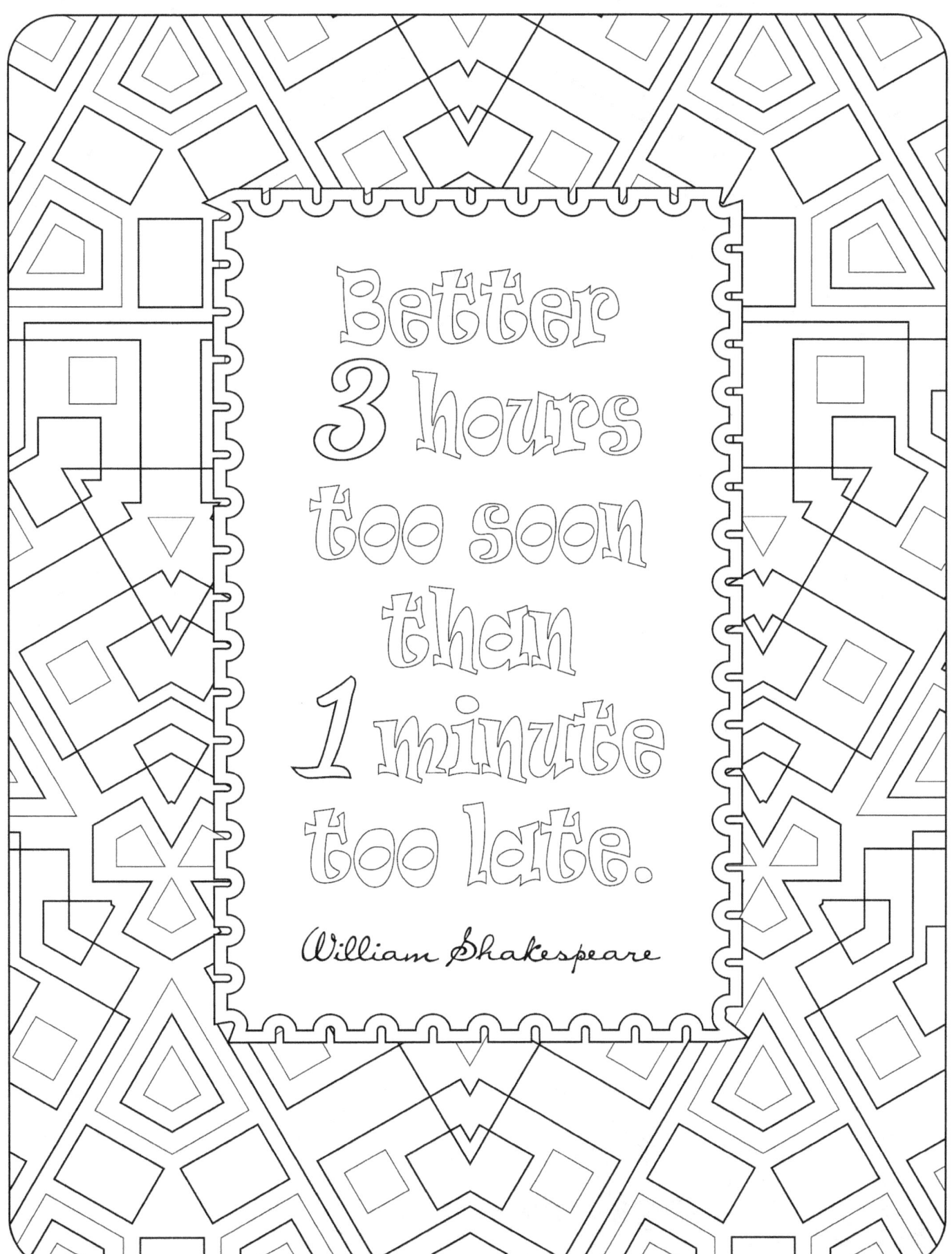

Better
3 hours
too soon
than
1 minute
too late.

William Shakespeare

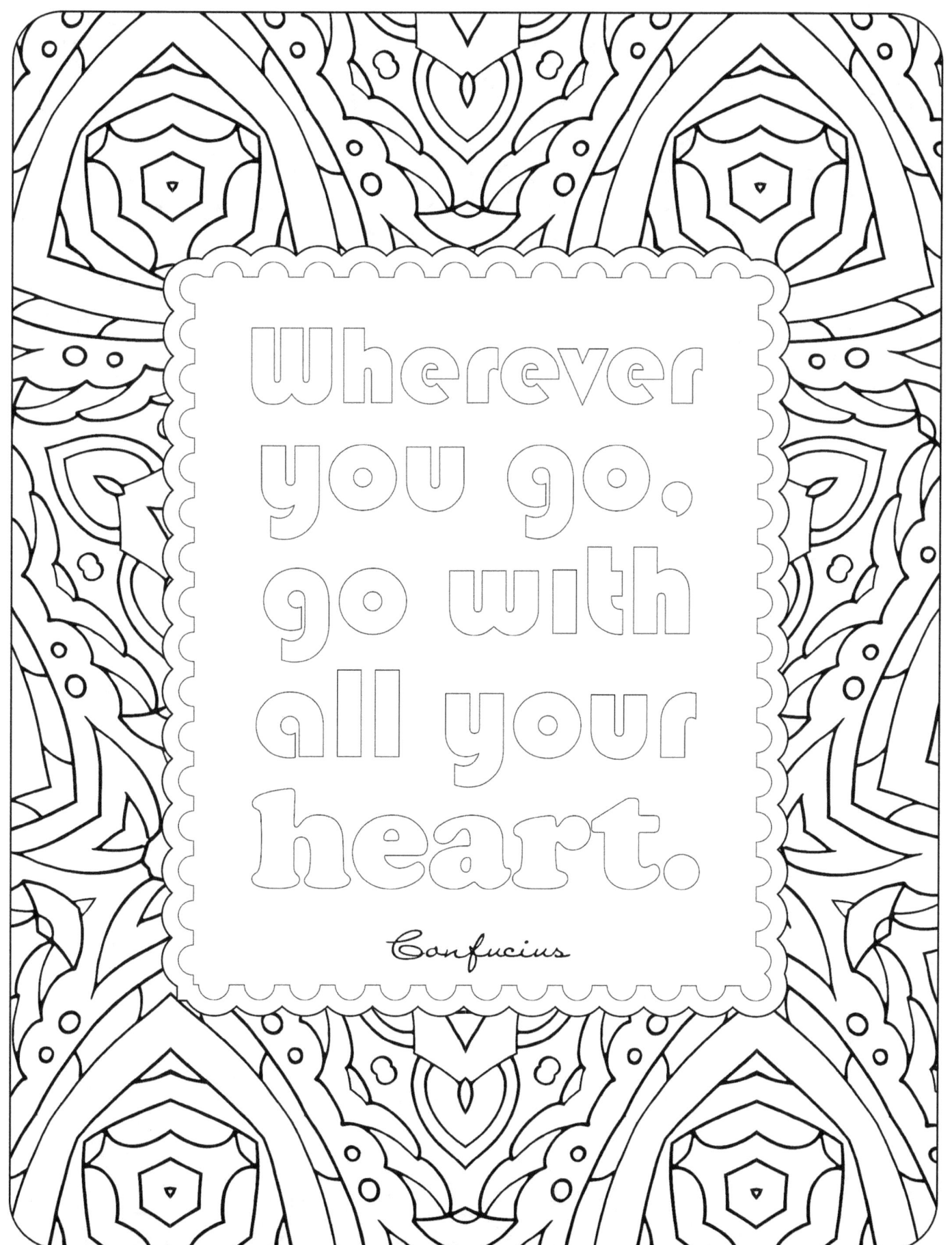

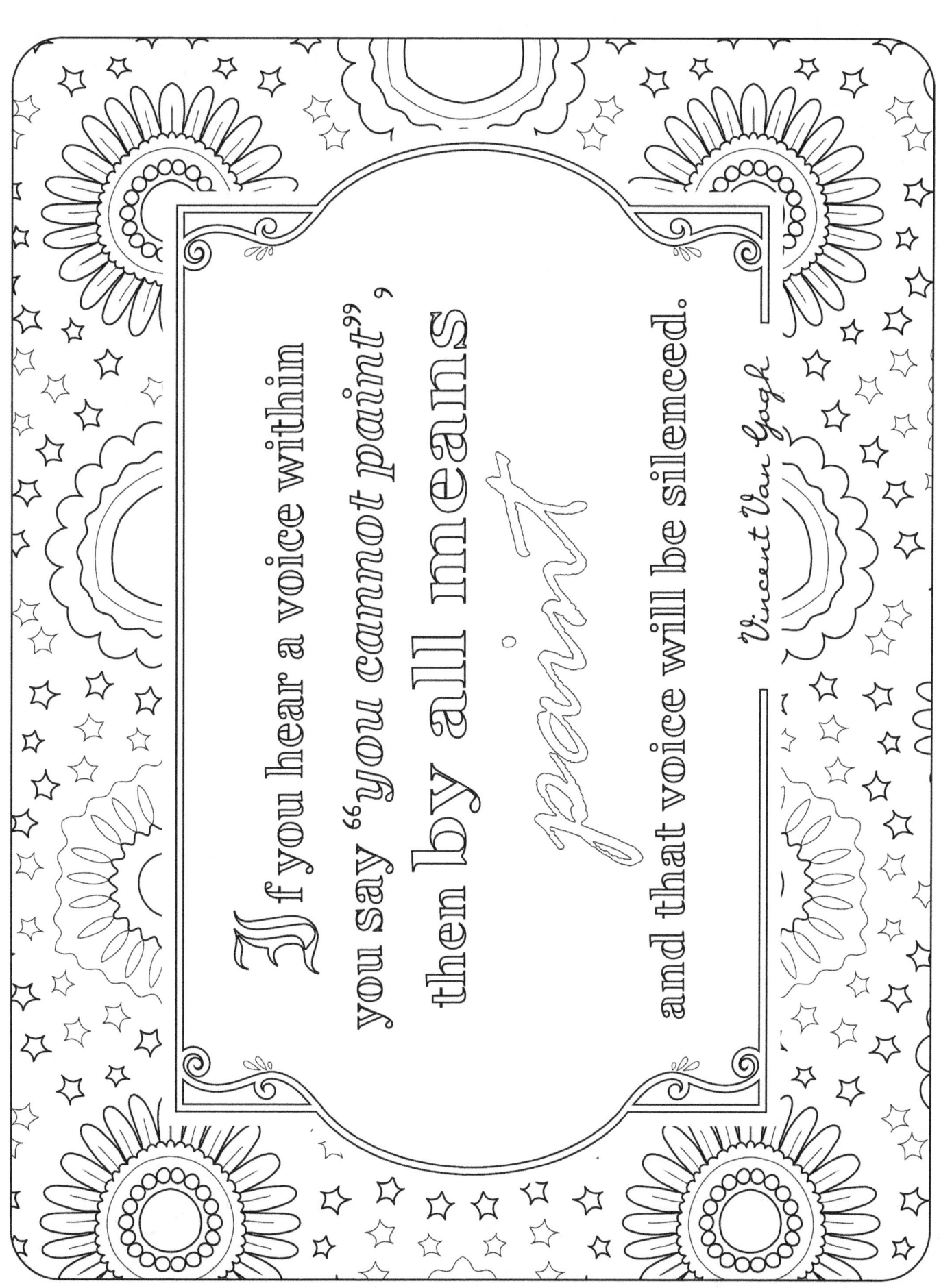

If you hear a voice within you say "you cannot paint", then by all means

paint

and that voice will be silenced.

Vincent Van Gogh

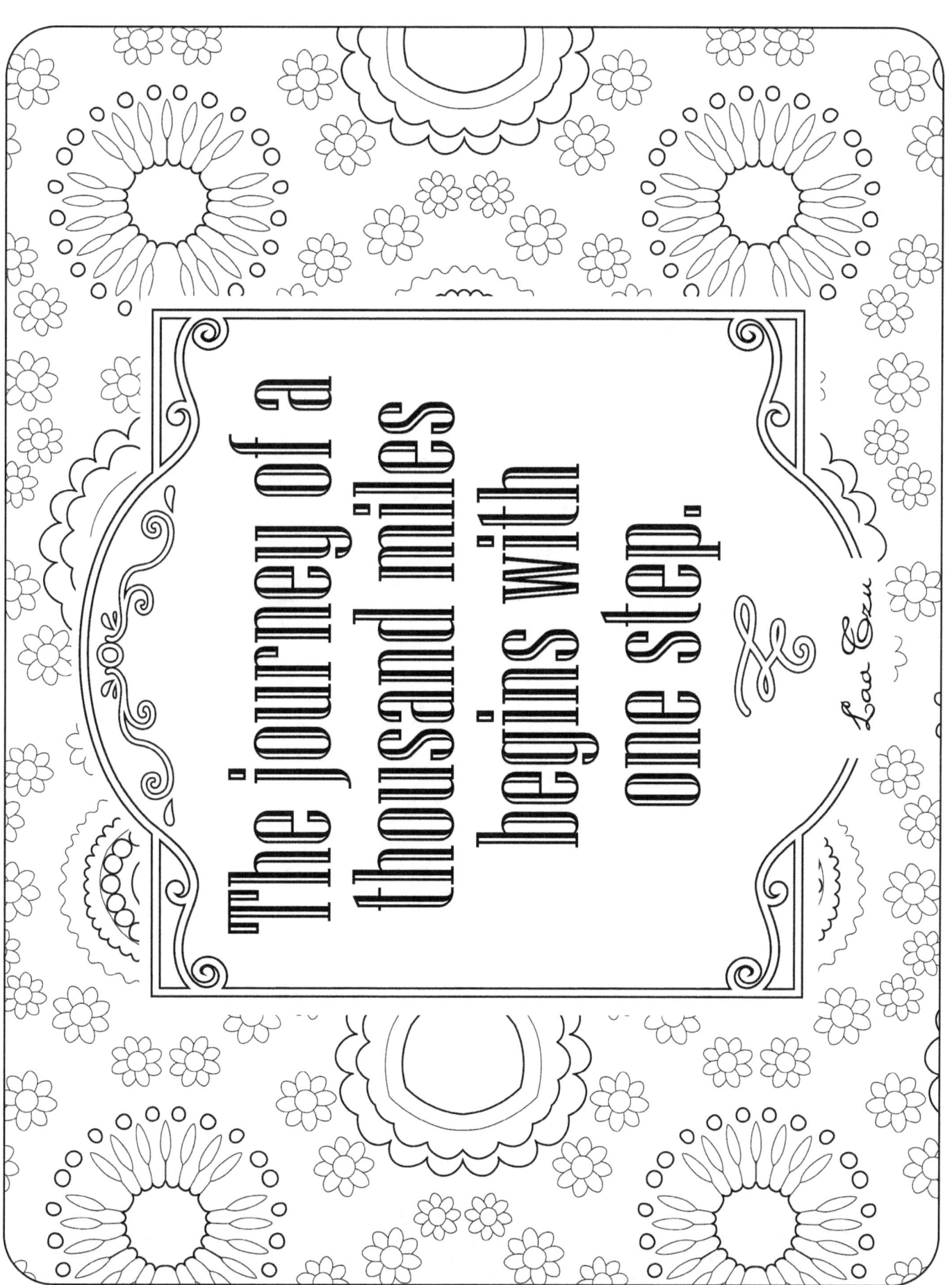

The journey of a thousand miles begins with one step.

Lao Tzu

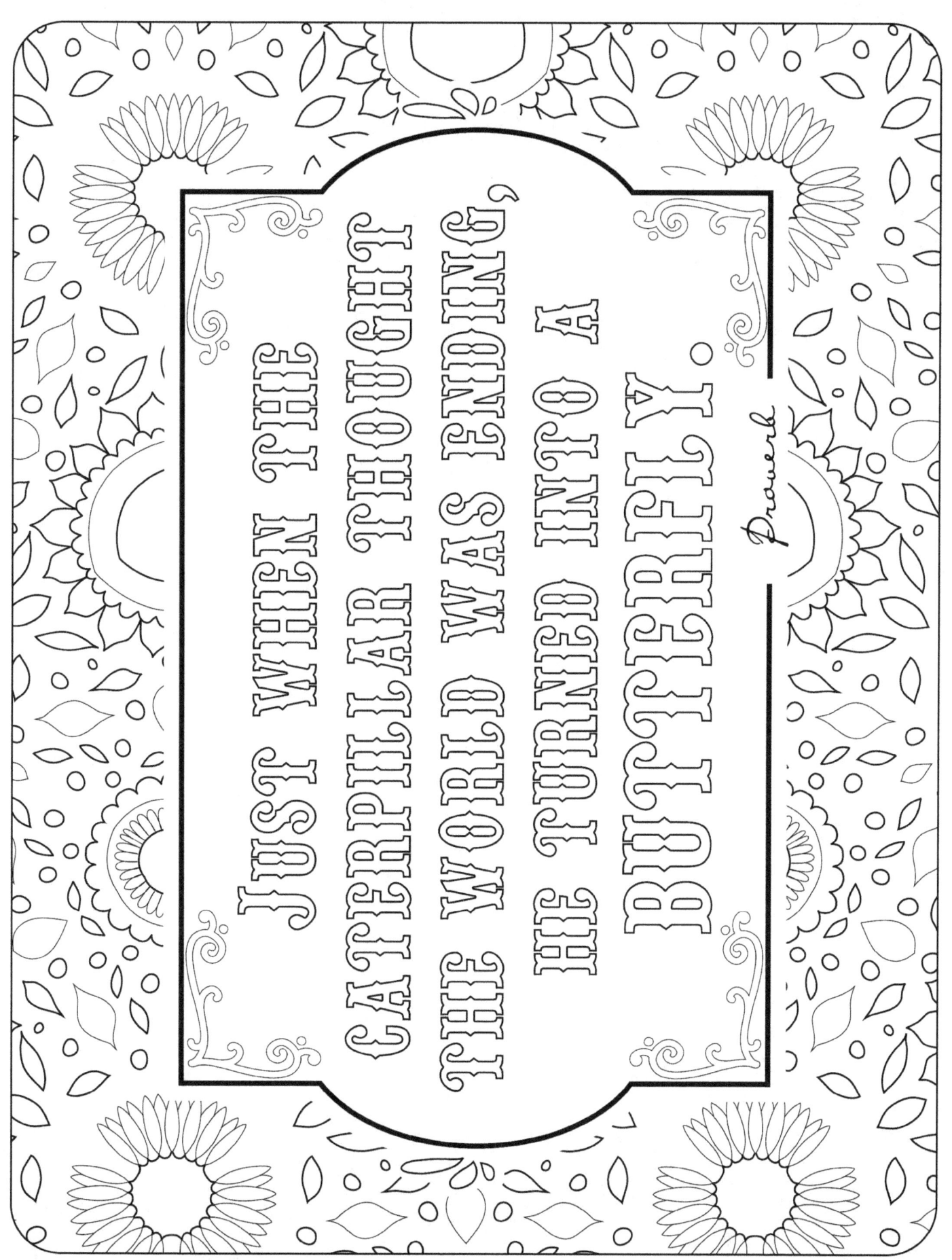

JUST WHEN THE CATERPILLAR THOUGHT THE WORLD WAS ENDING, HE TURNED INTO A BUTTERFLY.

Proverb

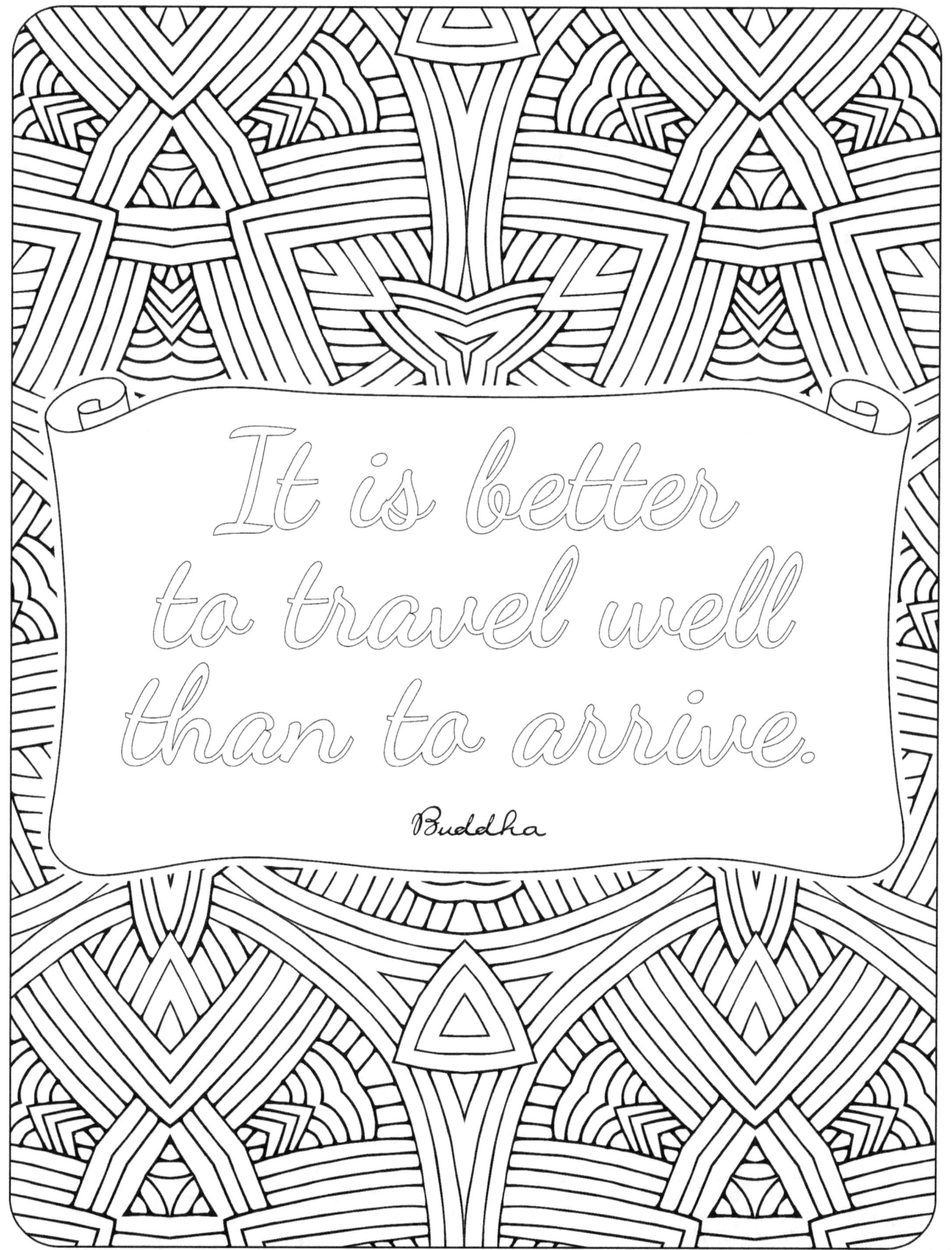

It is better
to travel well
than to arrive.

Buddha

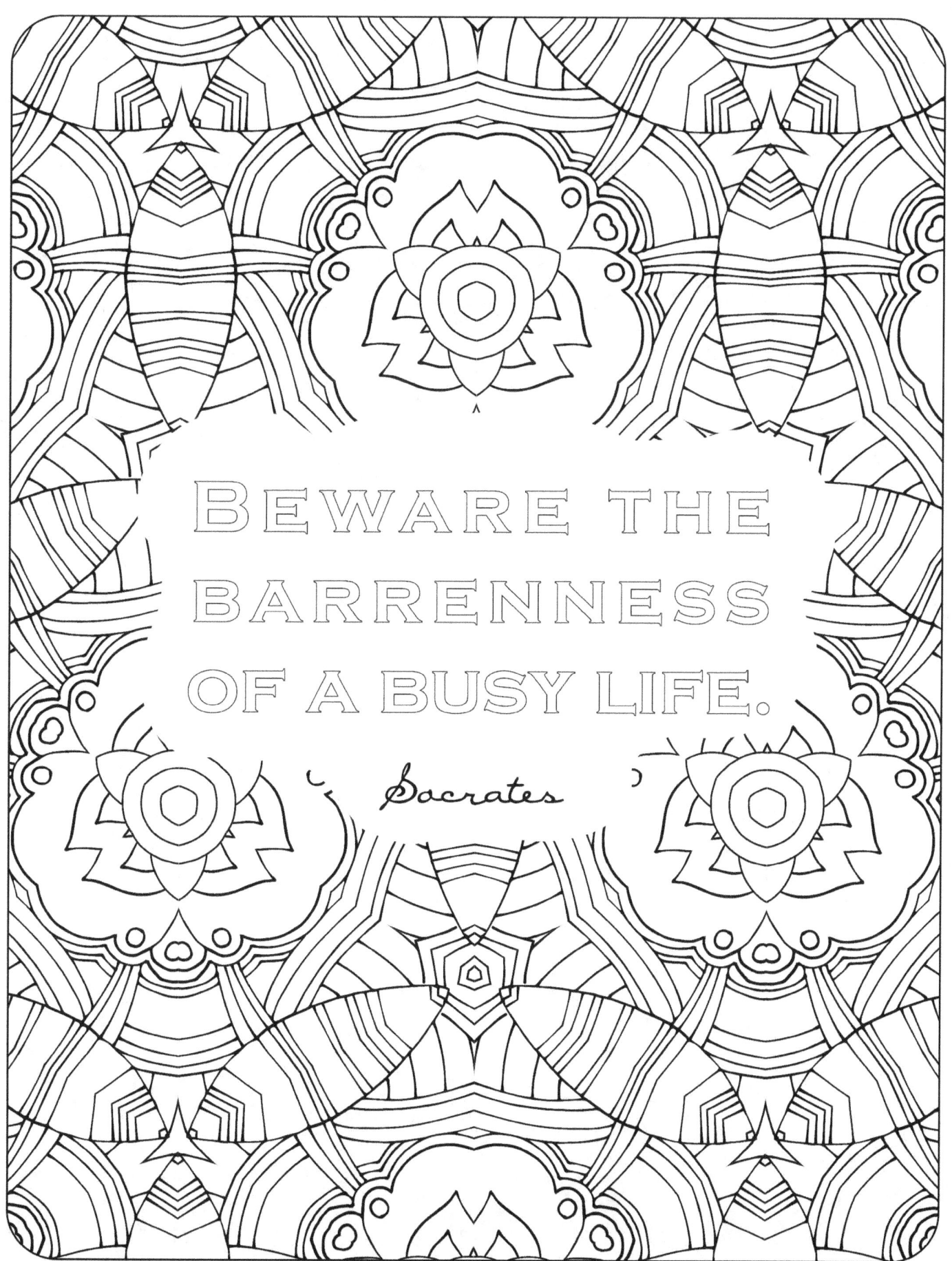

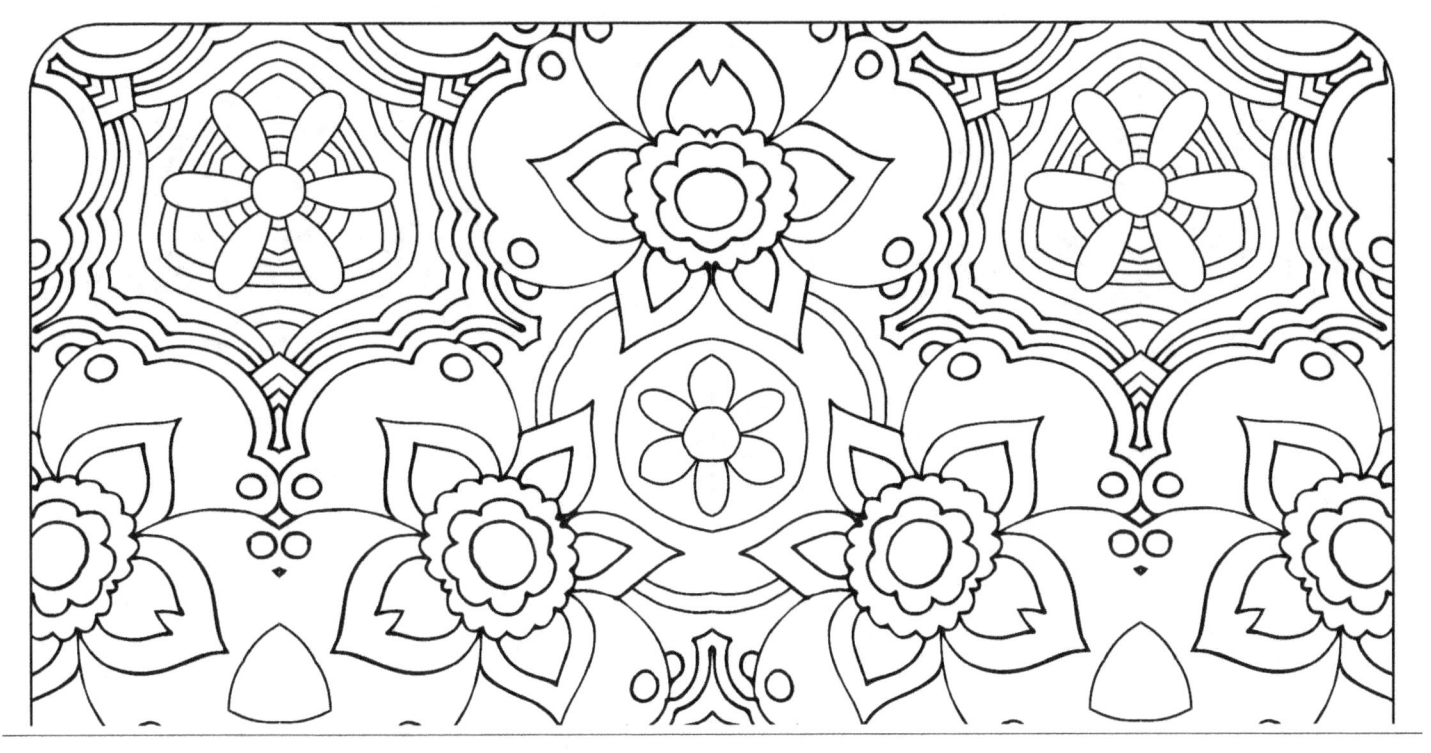

Self-respect knows no considerations.

— Mahatma Gandhi

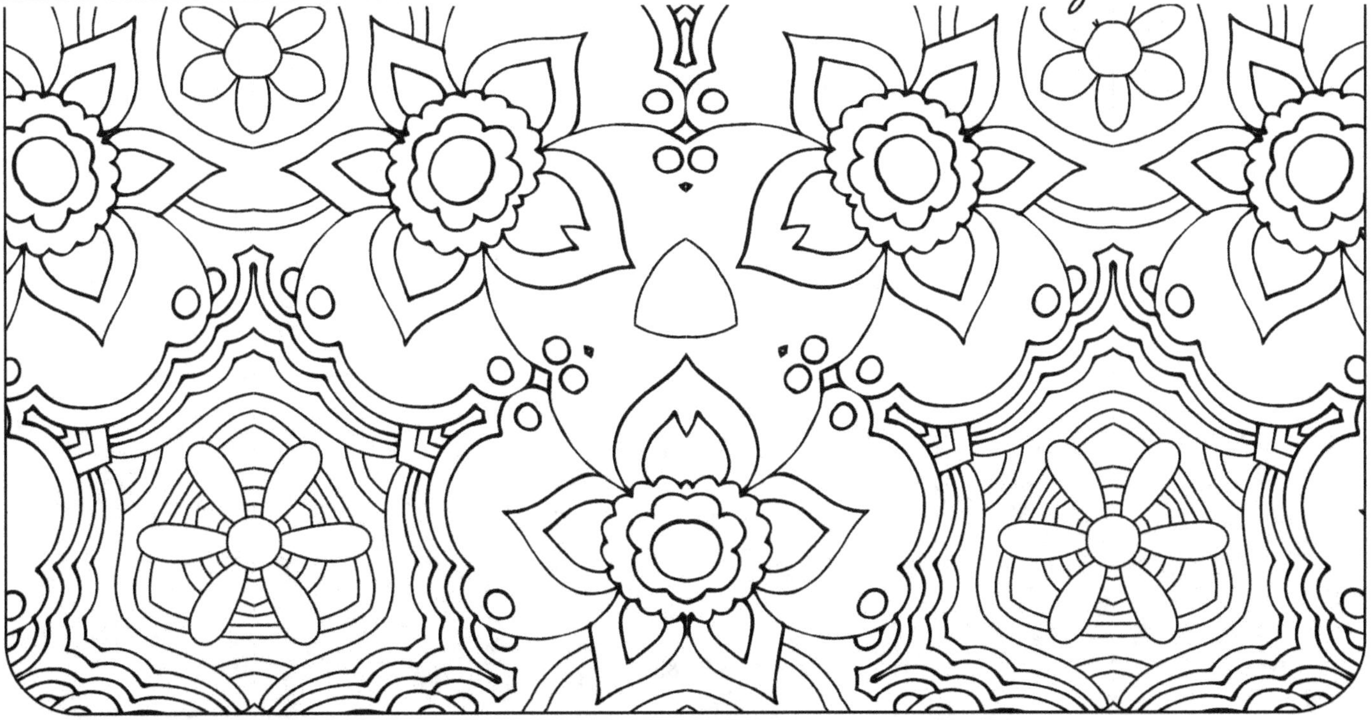

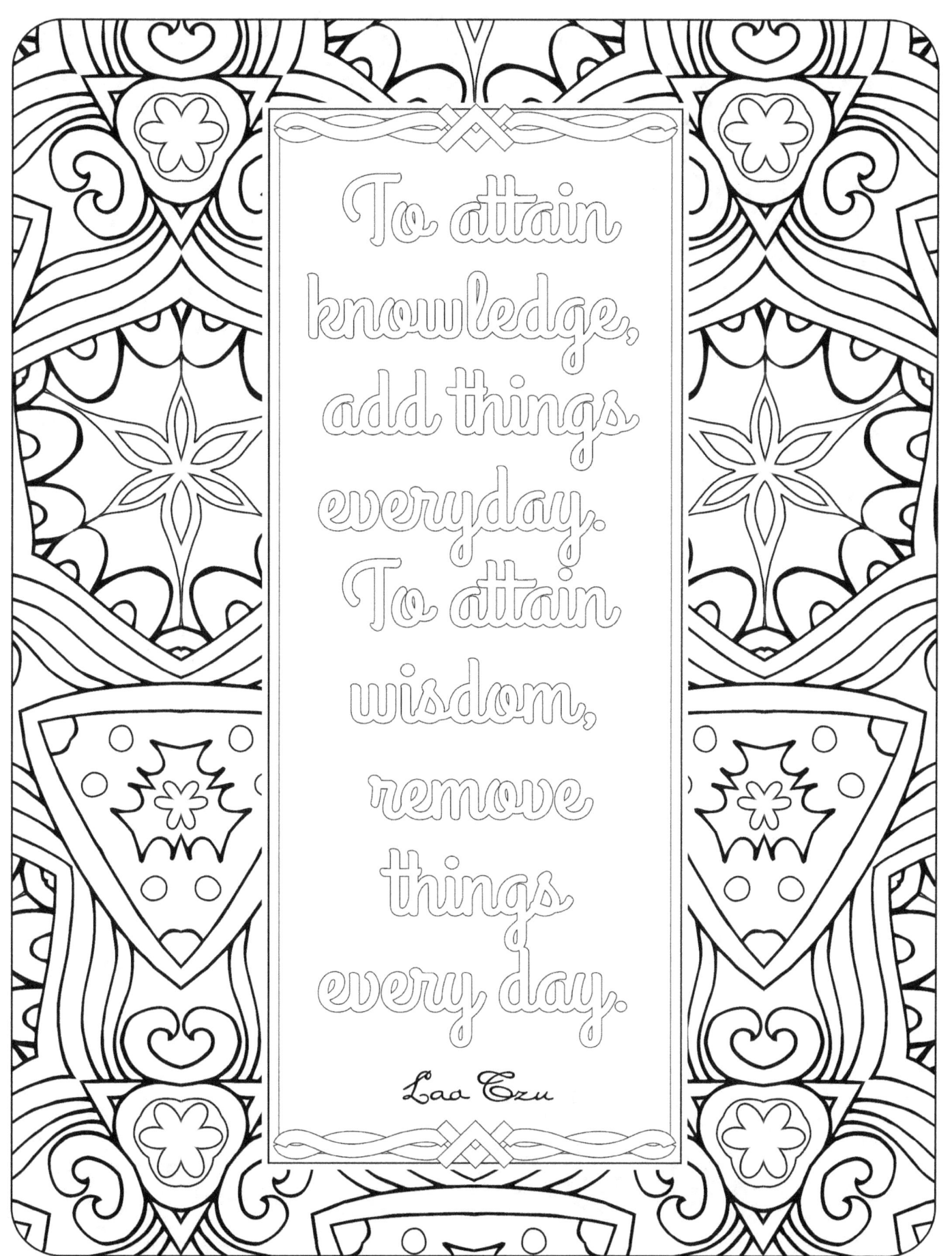

To attain knowledge, add things everyday. To attain wisdom, remove things every day.

Lao Tzu

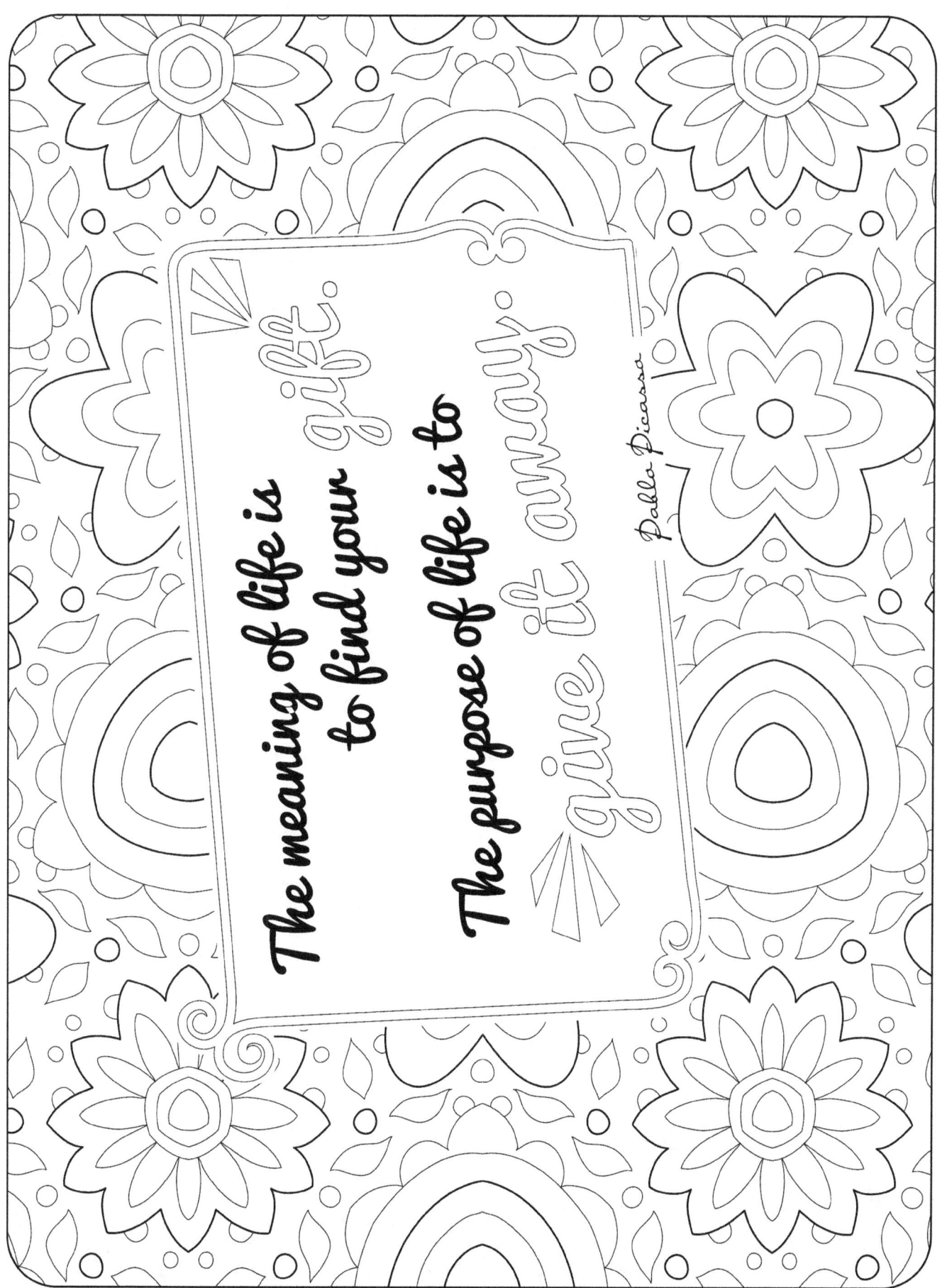

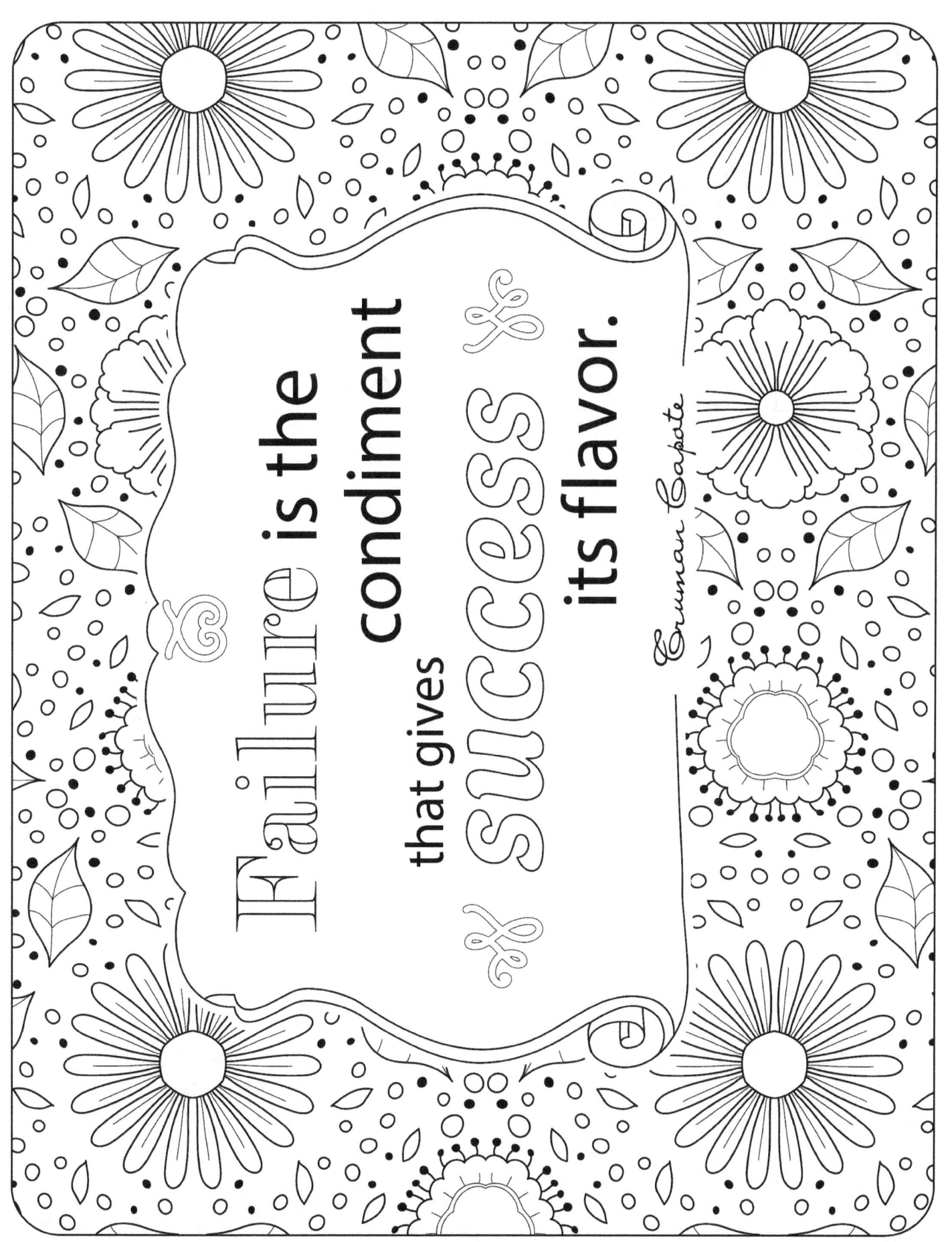

Failure is the condiment that gives SUCCESS its flavor.

Truman Capote

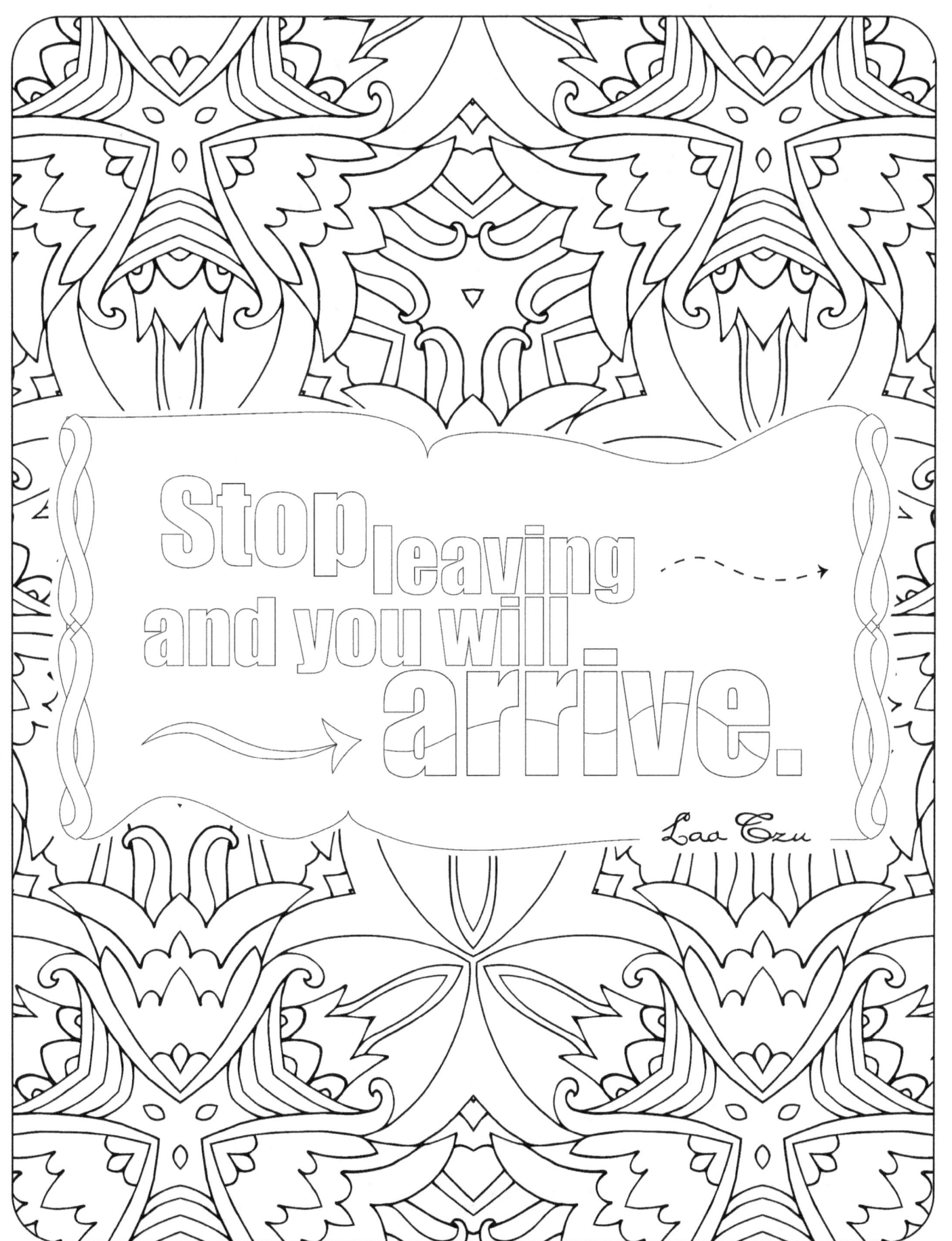

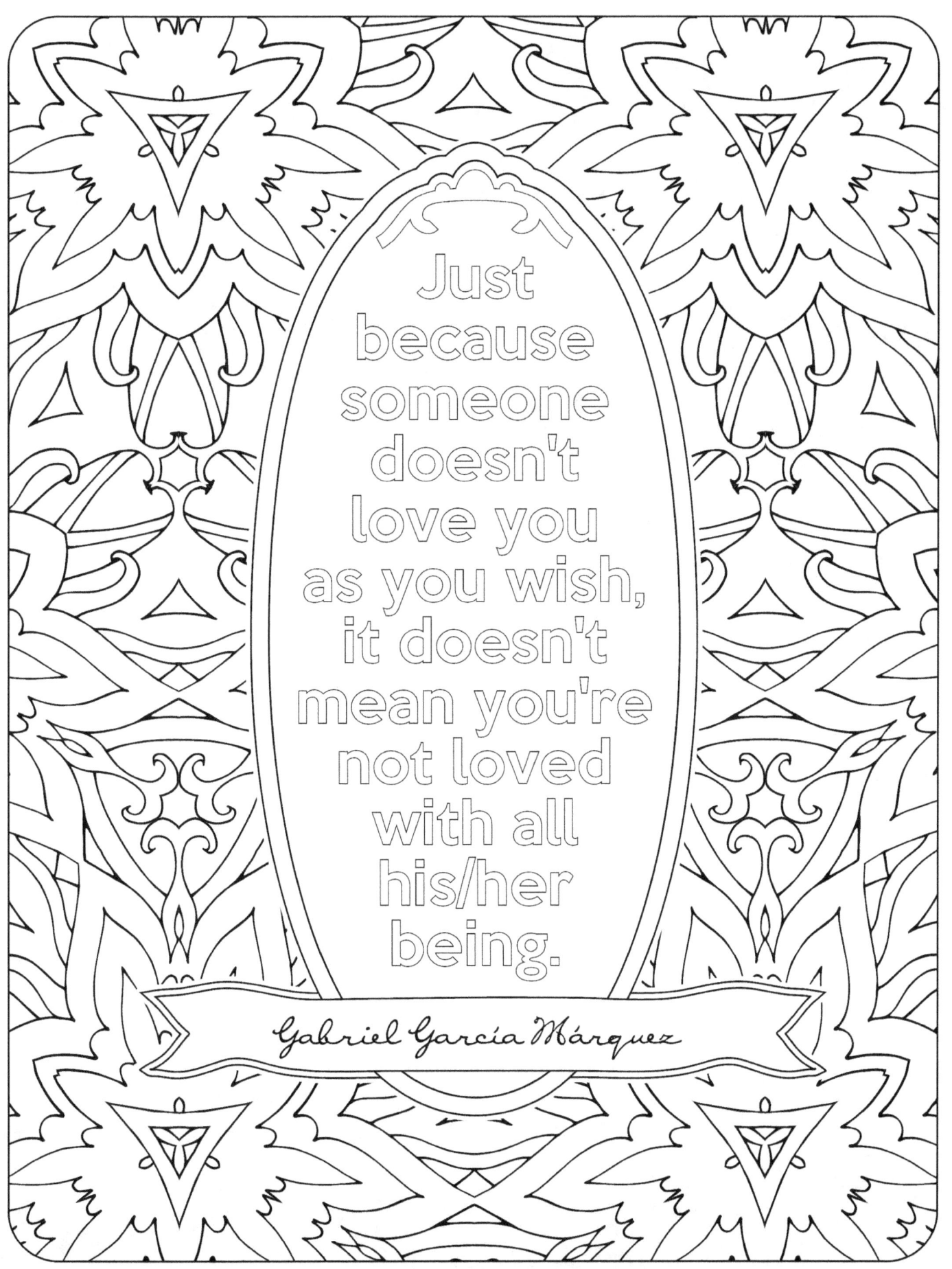

Just because someone doesn't love you as you wish, it doesn't mean you're not loved with all his/her being.

Gabriel García Márquez

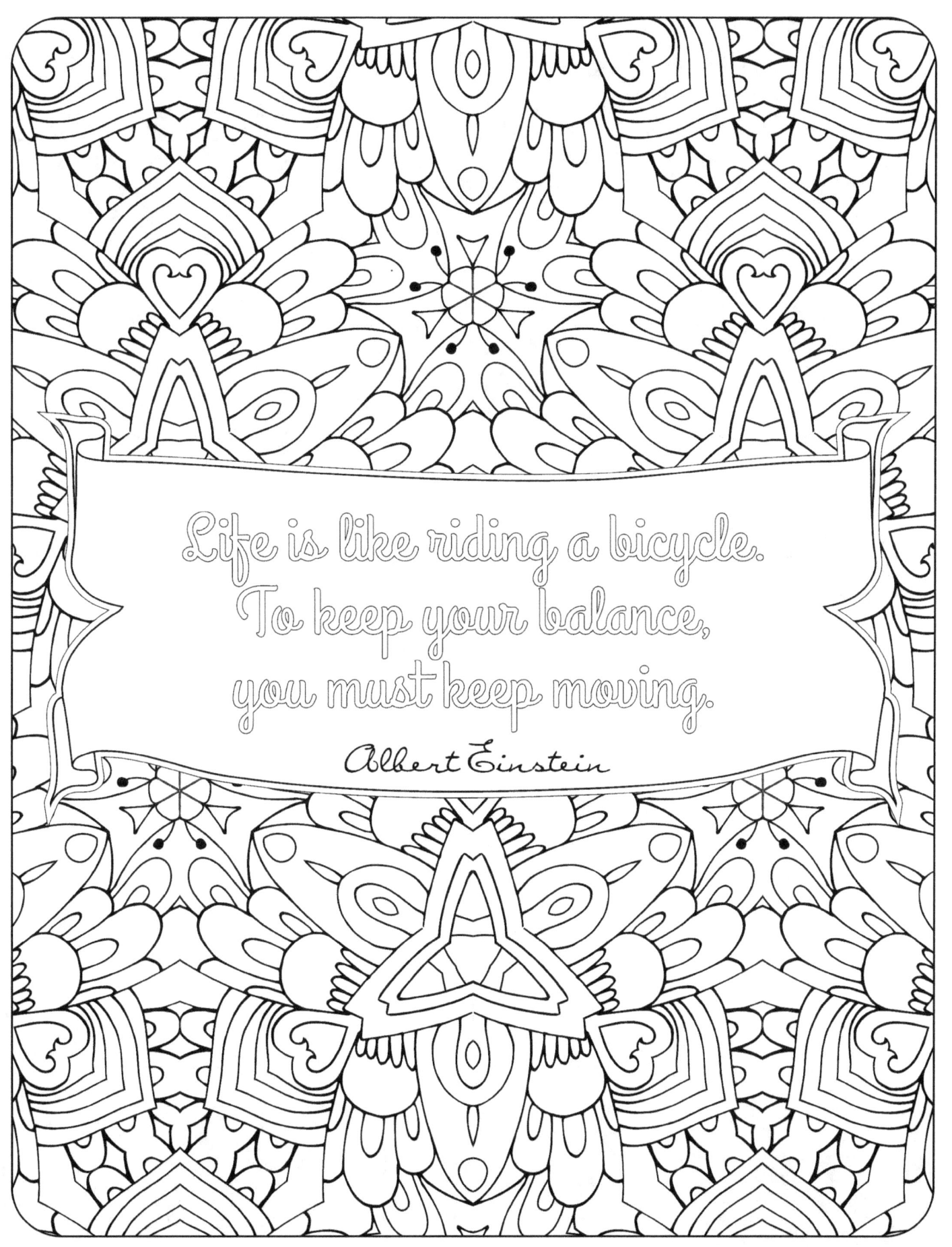

Life is like riding a bicycle.
To keep your balance,
you must keep moving.

Albert Einstein

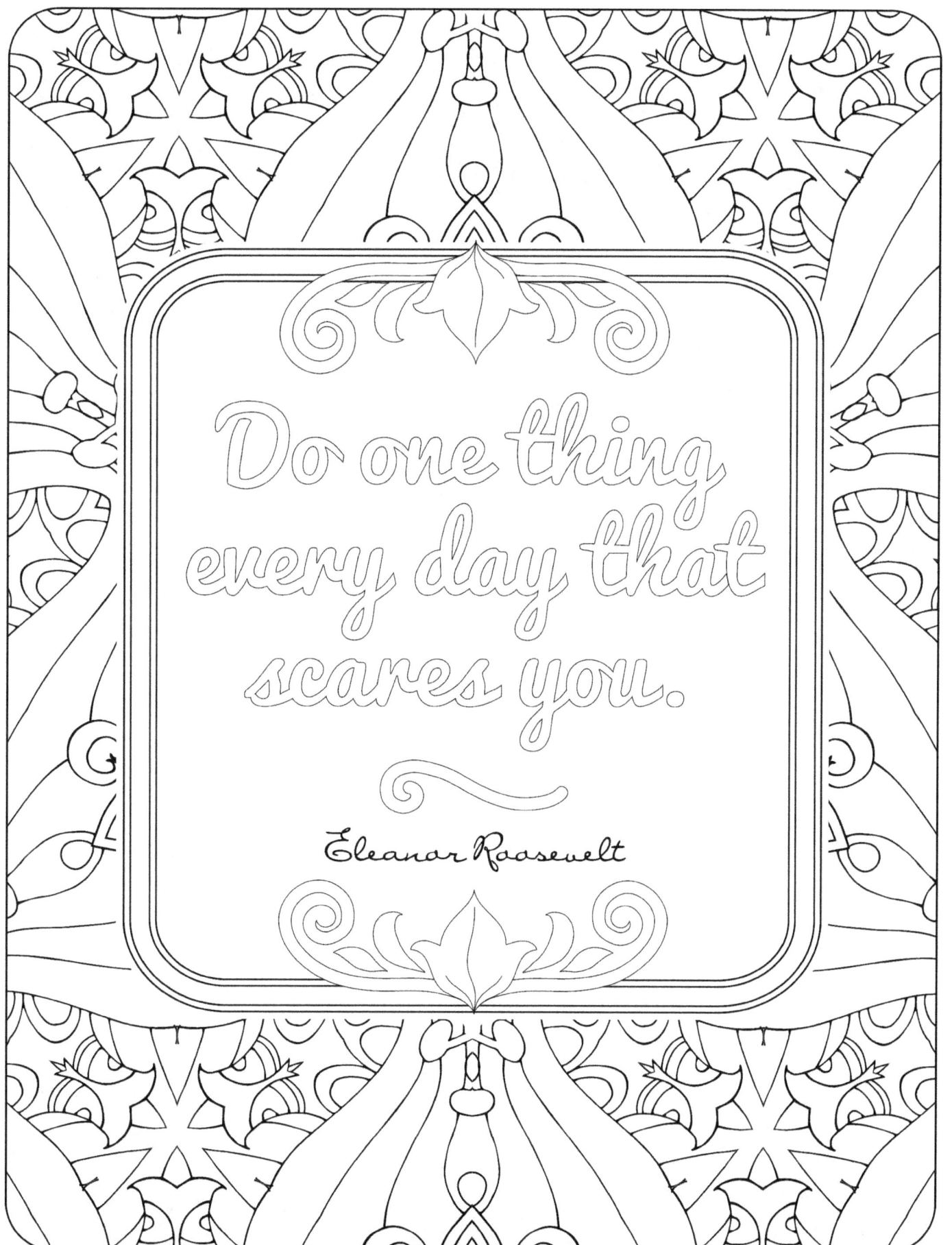

Do one thing every day that scares you.

Eleanor Roosevelt

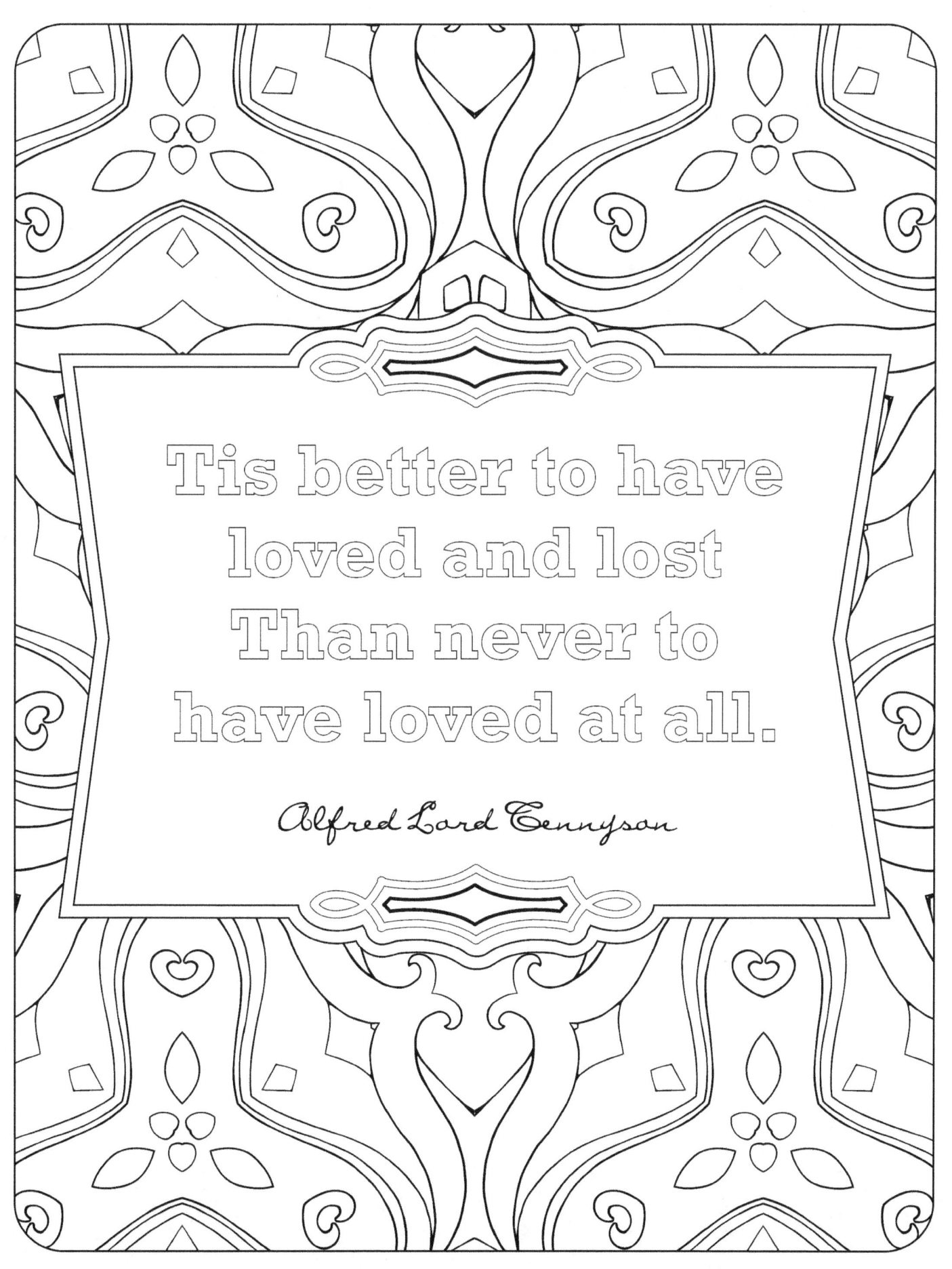

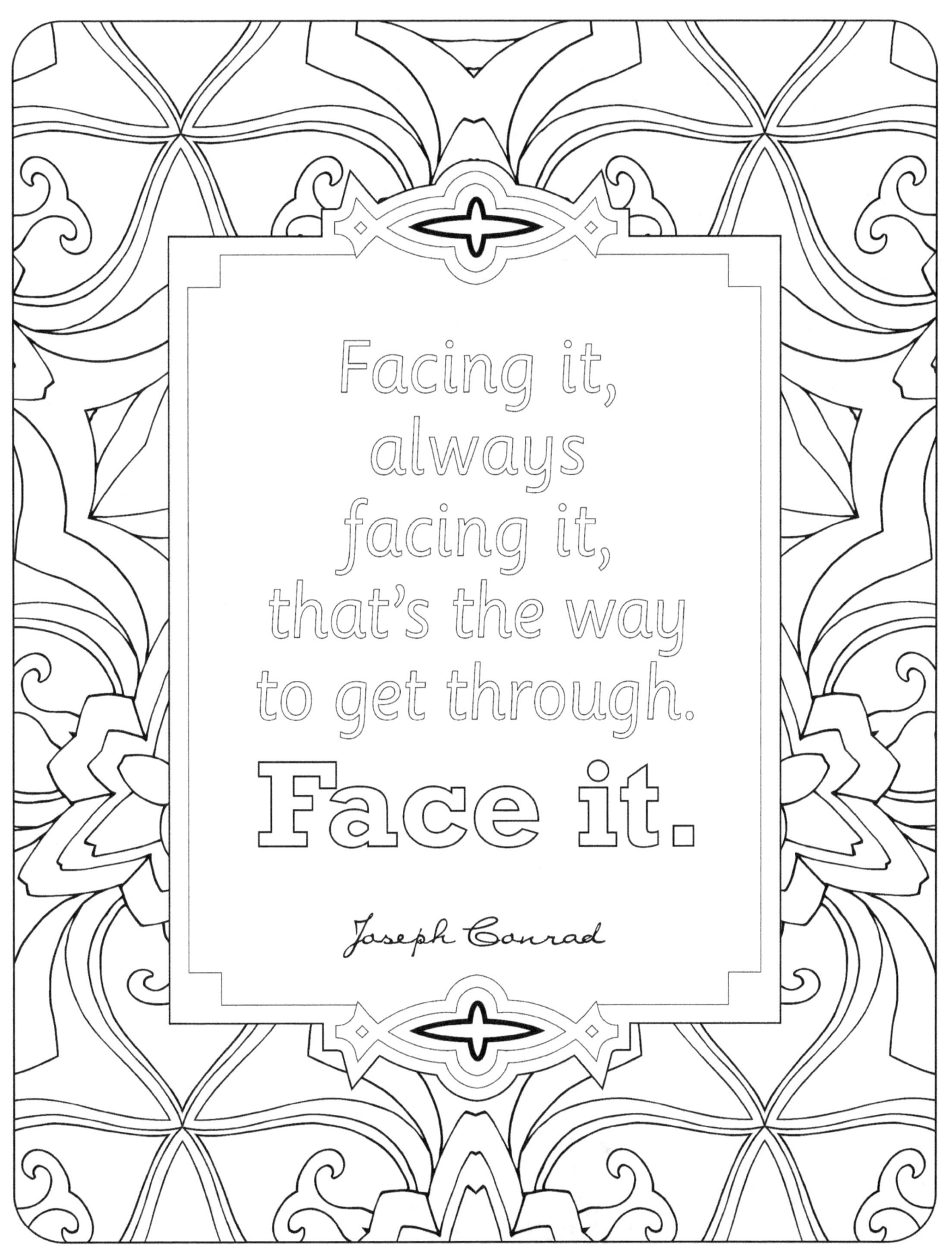

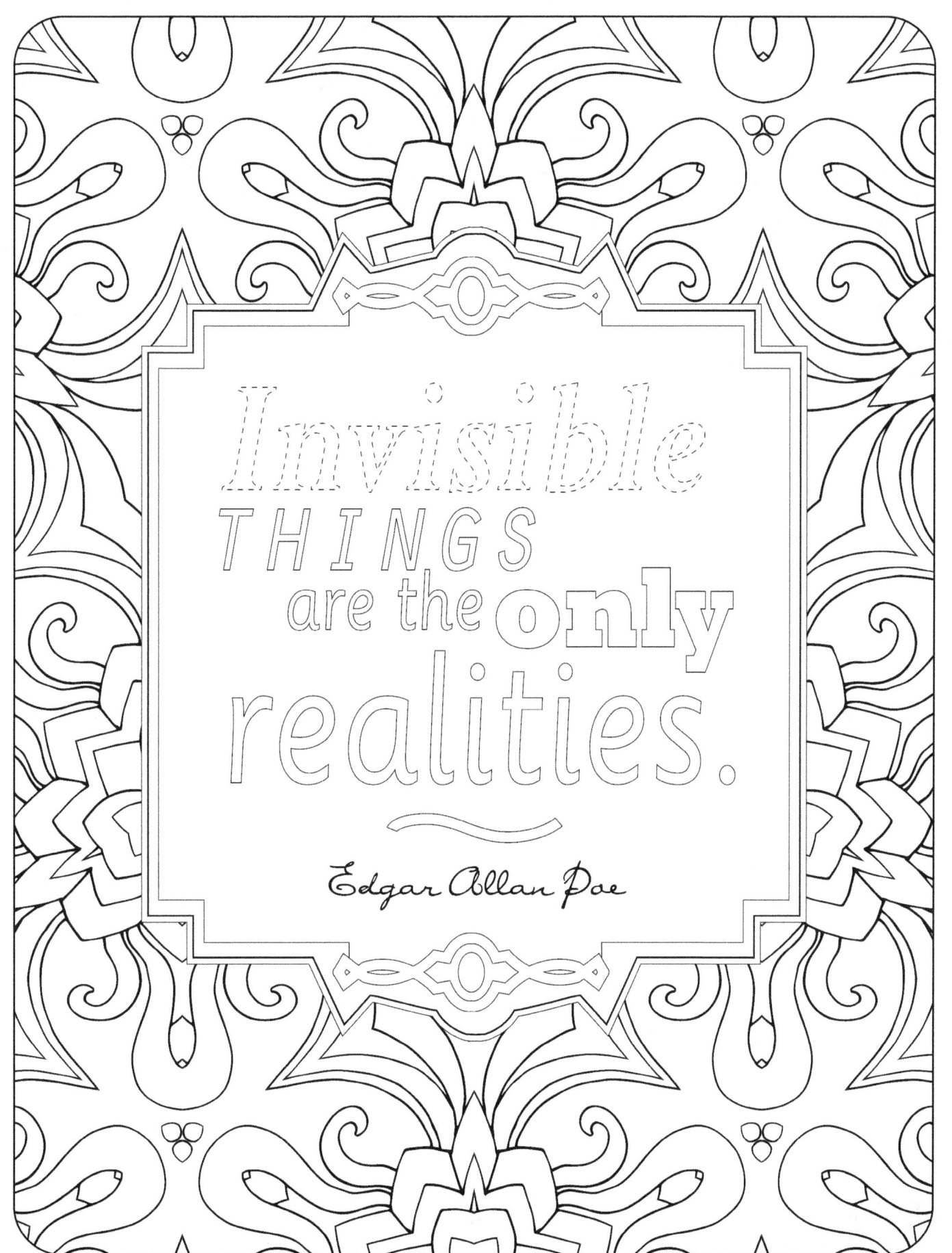

Invisible THINGS are the only realities.

— Edgar Allan Poe

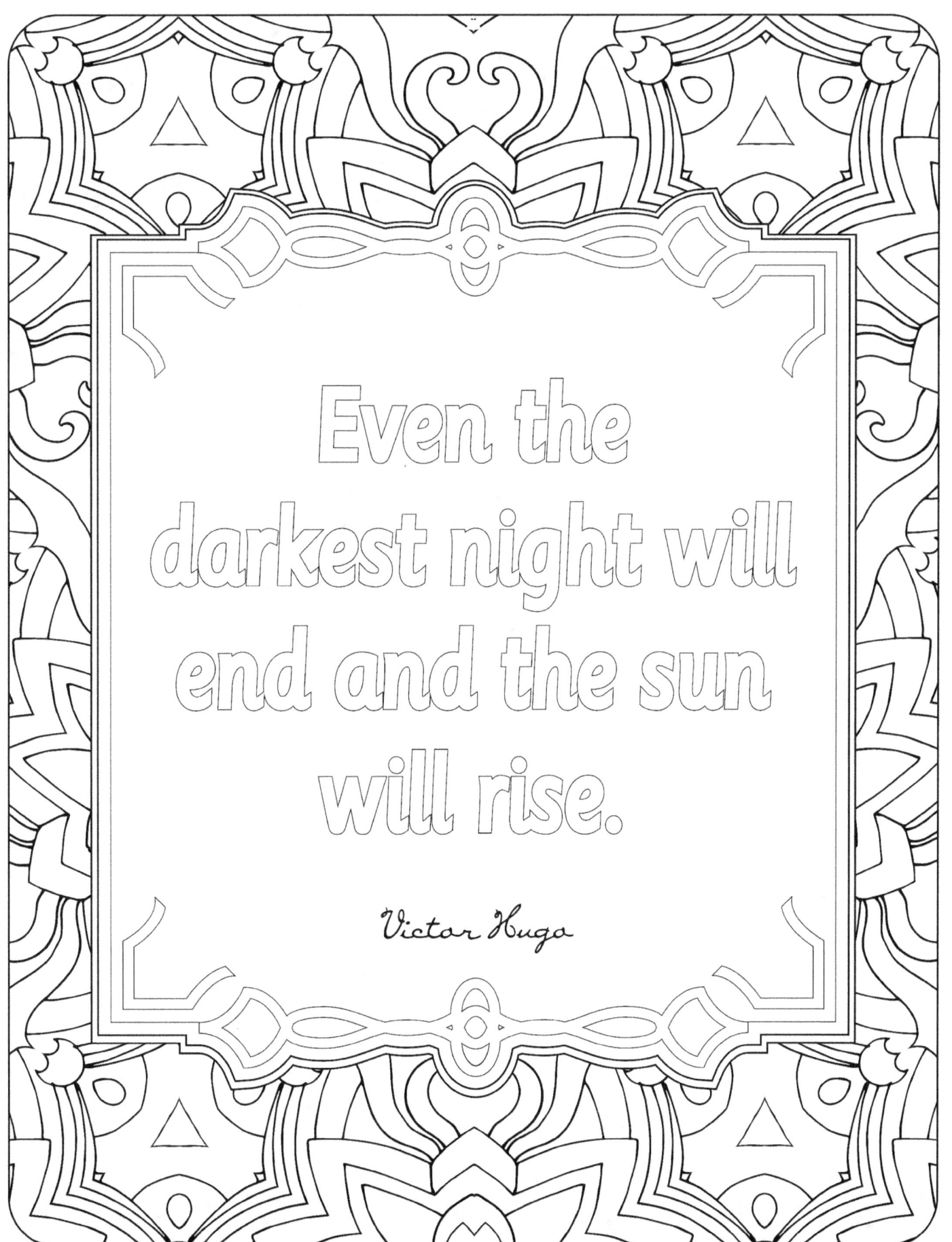

COLOR WITH US

www.LovinkColoring.com

Visit our website for more exclusive coloring pages or books